What They Need to Hear

What They Need to Hear

SHARING CHRIST with Family and Friends

KLEMET I. PREUS

CONCORDIA PUBLISHING HOUSE • SAINT LOUIS

Published by Concordia Publishing House
3558 S. Jefferson Avenue, St. Louis, MO 63118-3968
1-800-325-3040 • www.cph.org

Manufactured in the United States of America

Library of Congress Cataloging-in-Publication Data

Preus, Klemet I.
What they need to hear : sharing Christ with family and friends / Klemet I. Preus.
pages cm
ISBN 978-0-7586-3953-0
1. Witness bearing (Christianity) 2. Apologetics. 3. Evangelistic work. 4. Christianity. 5. Theology, Doctrinal. I. Title.

BV4520.P7155 2013
248'.5--dc23

2013000776

---

1 2 3 4 5 6 7 8 9 10 22 21 20 19 18 17 16 15 14 13

THIS BOOK IS DEDICATED TO LLOYD'S DAUGHTERS,
THE BINGAMAN SISTERS:

Dorita, Linda, Jan, Deb, and Liz

◇◇◇◇

Preface

Letters to Lloyd

On Epiphany, Sunday morning, January 6, 2008, Lloyd Bingaman died. The onslaught of cancer and ninety-two years of life had done their worst to my father-in-law, Lloyd. Eighteen months earlier, I had visited him at his home in Fresno, assuming that this would be our last conversation. Since he was dying, I decided I would talk to him about his faith. "Lloyd, it looks like you may die in the next few days or weeks. What are your thoughts about death?" Thus began a conversation that rambled through all sorts of topics relating in some way to the Christian message, eventually leading to this book.

Lloyd Bingaman had been baptized in a river at age ten. In his twenties he had been instructed into the teachings of the Lutheran Church and had joined that church when he married his wife, Edith. In the early years he had regularly attended services, but as his daughters grew up and left home, his commitment to the church decreased. After Edith died, he severed his relationship with any congregation. He didn't have any animosity toward the Church. He had even visited the church I pastored on occasion. He thought about God a lot, and we had had some interesting theological discussions over the years. He just didn't attend worship services or show much interest in wanting what Christ and the Church have to offer.

During our conversation it became apparent that Lloyd was uncertain of what was going to happen upon his death. He understood that if there were a place like heaven, then it would take a miracle for him to get there. Being mysteriously transported to the arms of Jesus upon the cessation of life is a miracle. Lloyd candidly admitted that he did not believe in miracles. He was especially skeptical about the veracity of the biblical account of the virgin birth of Christ. So I asked, "Lloyd, I know that you used to believe in miracles. You went to church. You took the Sacrament. You heard the stories. I know you used to believe."

He nodded agreement.

"So, what happened? Why did you stop believing?"

"I prayed to God that He would strengthen my faith, and He just didn't answer me," was his instant reply.

"Lloyd, you went about it all wrong. You prayed for faith, but that is not where faith comes from. 'Faith comes from hearing, and hearing through the Word of Christ' (Romans 10:17). If you wanted God to increase your faith, you should have listened to His Word." I wasn't so sure it was wise to correct Lloyd on his deathbed, but I felt I needed to point Lloyd to the promises of God, not his own prayerful strivings.

He then gave me a look as if to say, "Well, this is great. I want faith. It comes from the Word. I'm about to die, and where am I supposed get this 'Word' at this point? I can't go to church. I'm hardly even able to read anymore. How am I supposed to hear the Word? You're going back to your home tomorrow and I am helpless to get the Word."

So I answered his unarticulated questions. "Lloyd, if I were to write to you about Jesus a couple times a week for the rest of your life, would you read the letters?"

"Yes."

As it turned out, Lloyd lived another eighteen months, and I wrote him ninety-one letters. They were my attempt to tell someone who was not a Christian about Jesus. Thankfully, the Lord worked through these letters, and by all accounts Lloyd became a Christian in the months before he died.

In the process of writing to a family member about Christ, certain lessons about sharing the Gospel with family and friends became apparent to me. They are:

- Evangelists speak to one person often.
- Evangelists answer questions.
- Evangelists know that they work better in an environment of trust.

- No matter how unpleasant, true evangelists will always correct false doctrine when necessary.
- Risky as it may seem, evangelists learn to speak the Law.
- Evangelists learn to speak what they know of Christ in a variety of ways.

These lessons seem daunting, but as with any unpleasant situation, we know that "with God all things are possible" (Matthew 19:26). The letters that follow can be a template for you to follow with your own Lloyd—that person in your life who is questioning God and the Church. Maybe you want to provide answers but feel uncertain about your abilities. Use the lessons I have learned and will share in the following pages. Pray for guidance, and God will be with you.

What Is a Miracle?

Letter 1

I thoroughly enjoyed talking to you the other day, Lloyd. I have been praying that God would preserve your life, and I am confident He will—at least long enough for me to tell you a bit about miracles.

We specifically discussed the virgin birth of Christ. But really it might be worth talking about all miracles. You said that the virgin birth of Jesus was highly improbable. I agreed and added that, in fact, the virgin birth and all miracles are simply impossible.

A miracle is not simply a wonderful event, such as childbirth or a beautiful sunset. But even more than that, a miracle is not simply something that is very unlikely. Winning the lottery is unlikely, but no one would call it a miracle. Rather, a miracle is something that defies or even breaks the normal laws of nature. It is contrary to the laws of nature that a young woman could conceive and give birth without having relations with a man. You need the union of an egg and sperm for conception to occur, and that simply was not the case with the recorded account of the virgin birth of Jesus.

If there are no miracles, then there could be no virgin birth. Neither could there have been changing water into wine, walking on water, healing the paralyzed, raising the dead, or any of the miracles that are claimed in the Bible. So the question of the virgin birth is really a question about miracles in general.

It's not honest to say that you have to suspend all rational thinking and common sense to believe in miracles. Unfortunately, some Christians talk this way. "Simply take it by faith," they say. "Don't try to understand it. Just accept it." But if God did not want us to understand these things, then why would He even bother to tell us or explain things to us? According to the biblical account in Luke 1, Mary was curious when she was told she would give birth even though she had not slept with a man. The news required some type of explanation. God did not reply, "You have to take it by faith and suspend all common sense and rationality." Rather, He explained, "The Holy Spirit will come upon you, and the power of the Most High will overshadow you; therefore the child to be born will be called holy—the Son of God" (v. 35). God knows that we need some understanding, some kind of explanation for things.

God has established certain laws of nature, such as the law of gravity or that water freezes normally at 32 degrees Fahrenheit. These laws are not like moral laws, which can be broken, as when people sin, but with certain negative consequences. Natural laws cannot be broken at all—except by a miracle. A miracle is an act that violates or goes contrary to these established laws of nature. It stands to reason that the only one who can justly break a law is the one who established the law. So the only one who can break the laws of nature is the one who established those laws—namely God.

If anyone—you or I, for example—could work a miracle, then there would be miracles happening all the time, whenever it was convenient. If I could work a miracle, Lloyd, I would simply speak the word from a distance and give you back the health you had six months ago. But I can't do that. In fact, if I could work a miracle, I would just keep myself living eternally, and I would do the same for you. Then this entire discussion about miracles and God would not be needed! But I can't, so here goes.

Because only God can work a miracle, saying that miracles don't exist implies that either God doesn't exist or that He simply doesn't do miracles. I'm certain that you said that you believe there is a god. Since you are skeptical about miracles, that would suggest that you believe that God is just not in the business of breaking His own laws of nature by doing miracles.

◇◇◇◇

Still Skeptical about Miracles?

Letter 2

It makes sense to be skeptical about miracles. How sensible would it be for God to establish laws of nature and then go breaking them all the time? Why make laws if you aren't going to abide by them? If God were to break the laws of nature all the time, then how would we even know these laws? And if we couldn't learn the laws of nature, then we really wouldn't know when they were being broken. So, the only way to assert a miracle is to admit that miracles happen infrequently. They are, by nature, rare and unusual. God would only break His laws of nature if He had an exceptionally good reason to do so. It also makes sense to be skeptical about any claims that God has worked miracles to save lives or to prosper people in some way. Why would God make such exceptions to His rules? He certainly has the power to do so; I just don't know why He would. So miracles are very rare.

But let's say that by breaking a rule of nature God could actually do something that had lasting benefits for all people. And let's say that this was the only way in which God could accomplish these lasting benefits. Then wouldn't it make sense that God, if He cares about us at all, would break His own rules, especially if it was the only way to love us?

You might say "no" to these questions. You might believe that there is a god but that he never does any miracles. If that is the case, then you accept a god who never does anything that only God can do. (Since only God can do miracles.) But to believe in such a god is not sensible because the only way that you would know that there is a god is if he did something that no one else could do.

Let me give an example. Only a loon makes that unique and mournful sound on the lake in the evening. I trust you have heard it. What if I said that there was a loon on the lake, though no one has ever heard his sad song or seen him? To assert that there is a loon on the lake I must have some indication either by sight or sound. Something must have occurred that only loons can do. It's the same with God. If you say that God exists, you must have some indication of God by seeing either Him or what He has done. If there have never been any miracles (and we assume that you have not seen God), then you really can't claim that there is a god. If you believe there is no god, then we can have a different discussion. But, since you believe that God exists, then it only makes sense that God can do, and has done, miracles. Otherwise either He is not really God, or you have no way of knowing that He exists.

It is essential to believe that miracles are quite rare, otherwise you could never know what is natural and normal. And it is essential to believe that miracles have occurred, otherwise you would have no way of knowing that God exists.

Miracles Are Necessary

Letter 3

Miracles are necessary for two reasons. The first reason, as I told you previously, is that miracles are necessary in order for us to believe in God. If there had never been a miracle in the history of the world until now, then why would we even think that God exists?

Let's say that someone billed me for cleaning my house, but I could see absolutely no indication that the house had been cleaned. Nothing had been straightened up. Nothing had been dusted or washed. There was no indication that anyone had stepped over the front door threshold to clean. I would not pay the bill because I would not believe that anyone had even been there. So it is with God; if there is absolutely no indication in the whole world that He has been around, then why believe in Him at all? So there has to be some indication that God has been here for us to believe in Him.

It is reasonable to believe that God exists because there are plenty of indications. The reality of the universe is an indication that God intervened into nothingness and made something. Matter does not just happen. I think we could call it a miracle that the universe was brought into being. It required establishing natural laws. If breaking natural laws is a miracle, then establishing these same laws is also a miracle. In fact, the existence of the universe requires the creation of nature itself. So, concluding that things got started by a miracle is concluding that miracles can happen and that God exists.

But let's say someone believes that things just came into being by accident and without the intervention of God, that the existence of the universe is not a miracle. Still, the ordered nature of the world also indicates some type of intervention. Scientists know that the inner balance of the world is so intricate and so delicate that the slightest variation of the way things are would cause a major catastrophe from which nothing would survive. The temperature rises five degrees and the whole world floods. A meteor comes too close to the earth. Gravity ceases to function and causes a worldwide skewing of gravity. Dozens of disaster movies are based on premises such as these. The likelihood of these events is impossible—or at least implausible. Scientists estimate that there would have had to have been literally millions of "big bangs" before there came into being an ordered universe from a specific big bang.

But let's suppose that we did have a million big bangs before the universe finally became ordered and balanced. Still, the spontaneous generation of life would have to happen in order for there to be any living beings. We know that there are living beings because one of them is reading at this very moment. And we all know that life does not spontaneously generate. In fact, when Elijah breathed life into the widow's deceased son, it was called a miracle (1 Kings 17:17–24). So I would say that if nature can breathe life into things that are not living, that is just as much a miracle. We have already established that only God can do a miracle. So, the existence of life must be a miracle since the normal laws of nature are broken in order for the first life to come into being.

The existence of the universe, the ordered design of the universe, and the fact that there is life all show that God exists. All these things are miracles. They do not happen naturally, just like my house is not ordered and cleaned spontaneously. They require the intervention of someone. This world—for us to accept it the way it is—requires belief that God has intervened with miracles.

◇◇◇◇

Miracles Are Necessary for Us to Be Redeemed

Letter 4

The New Testament writers believed that Jesus did miracles. They also believed that these miracles served important functions other than to just help people. God would not have needed to send Jesus into this world to die on the cross if all He wanted to do was simply "help" us.

Even if you don't believe that the miracles of the New Testament happened, you should at least understand why the biblical writers reported them. In the New Testament God is presented as doing something completely unique: coming into this world to save us.

So you have the good news that the little baby in Bethlehem is "Christ the Lord." Now, little babies are born in Bethlehem with some regularity. And even a little baby placed in a manger because there is no room in the inn, while charming, is nothing special. So how can God call our attention to this particular baby? He works a miracle. Remember that miracles are extremely rare, so this must be an extremely important event.

Imagine that you are presenting your children with an incredibly precious gift. Imagine that the value of the gift is not at all obvious. Would you just give it to your children? I doubt it. They might throw it away or waste it. They might store it in the back of the closet. So you would indicate in some manner that the gift had value. You would tell them, "This is much more precious than it seems." You would place the gift on a cushion. You would wrap it with ornate and expensive paper. You would do something.

God had something special to give. We may not have understood the importance of this little baby in a common manger, so God tells us. But He is not content to send just an angel or two. He sends the entire heavenly host. He appears to Wise Men. He speaks through Simeon who was the old man that circumcised Jesus. He speaks through John the Baptist who, like Jesus, had a miraculous birth. He speaks in all sorts of unlikely means.

Lloyd, if you say that there are no miracles, then you are taking away from God the one way He has to tell us that something very special is happening. Tomorrow, I will write more about the virgin birth of Christ, a miracle that many people have difficulty accepting.

◇◇◇◇

The Virgin Birth

Letter 5

The virgin birth of Christ (Matthew 1:18–25) is not impossible if God exists. No miracle is impossible for almighty God. Certainly the virgin birth breaks the normal laws of nature, as miracles do. But why would God bring Jesus into the world through a virgin birth?

Well, God had a job to do. He wanted to come into this world. He couldn't come with all His glory and splendor, or He would scare us. Seeing God face-to-face would kill us. (The angels in the field created a great deal of fear in the hearts of the shepherds [Luke 2:8–20]; think if God had shown up with all His glory!) God wants to come into this world in such a way that He will not scare us. He has to take upon Himself the flesh and blood of an ordinary man so that we will not flee. God wants to not only appear like a man, He also wants to be a man. He wants to subject Himself to all the limitations that the laws of nature place upon us. He wants to subject Himself to the moral laws of this world. Suppose God wants to be and to feel just like us. That means that He must come into this world as a newborn. He must grow from infancy to adulthood just like other humans must do.

But let's say, further, that God, who wants to come into this world as a man, is born of the normal union of a man and a woman. Well, how would anyone know that the little boy born in such a way was God? You and I were born of the normal and natural union of a man and a woman. Consequently, we have never claimed to be God. God, to come into this world as a man, has to come in a unique, miraculous manner. But He has to be fully human.

Therefore, Jesus was born of the Virgin Mary, who became pregnant without having relations with a man. It's a story that is predicted from the first pages of the Bible. God told Eve, not Adam, that she would give birth to a "seed" which would crush the serpent's head (Genesis 3:15). God told

Isaiah that "the virgin shall conceive and bear a son, and shall call His name Immanuel," which means "God is with us" (Isaiah 7:14). Matthew goes to great pains to show that Joseph had no relations with Mary until after Jesus was born (Matthew 1:24–25). The angel explains to the blessed Virgin that "the Holy Spirit will come upon you, and the power of the Most High will overshadow you; therefore the child to be born will be called holy—the Son of God" (Luke 1:35). Later in the New Testament, Paul says, "when the fullness of time had come, God sent forth His Son, born of a woman, born under the law, to redeem those who were under the law, so that we might receive adoption as sons" (Galatians 4:4–5). Notice there is no reference to Jesus being born of a man. His birth was of a woman. It places Him under the law. And it shows Him to be God's Son.

If you say that the virgin birth can't happen, then you are saying that God cannot come into this world to intervene in our lives. You are saying that God cannot become a flesh-and-blood man in order to live in our space, breathe our air, suffer our existence, and redeem us. Without a virgin birth, God is stuck in heaven, can't come to earth, and never the twain shall meet. It's a sobering, depressing thought, Lloyd. But if there really was a virgin birth? Well, that's a story for tomorrow.

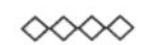

The Meaning of the Virgin Birth

Letter 6

If miracles require the intervention of God, then the miracle of the virgin birth is doubly significant. Not only does the virgin birth indicate that God has intervened, it also indicates that God Himself has come into this world as a man. Theologians call this the incarnation (taking on flesh); everyone else calls it Christmas.

For God to take on flesh He must have had a pretty good reason. The reason, simply, is His love. Here is God's plan:

- He created us pure and lovely, sinless, and without flaws. The Bible uses the word *good* (Genesis 1:10) to describe God's view of creation.
- Our first parents, and every person since, have acted selfishly. We have not placed God first in our devotion and we have not placed others first in our service. Instead, we have been devoted primarily to ourselves. It's an ego-driven world. We are, in fact, so ego-driven that we have lost the ability truly to live for others.
- God became angry—angry because we corrupted the freedom and love that He intended for us. People have an inevitable tendency toward the slavish and unloving habits of selfishness. This was most certainly not God's intention.

- God destroyed the world with a flood. He rejected all but a chosen, unlikely people: the Jews. On this chosen people He lavished great attention and blessing. Still, His chosen people were the most stubborn of all peoples. He threatened, cajoled, admonished, urged, and otherwise tried to bring His people back to Himself. He wanted nothing more than for them to return to the pristine affections that they showed in the beginning. Nothing improved their behavior.
- Finally, God decided that He would come into the world Himself. He would do two things. First, He would submit Himself to His own will and obey it. He would count this obedience to our credit. That required that He became a flesh-and-blood man. Second, He would absorb the selfishness and sin that characterized His people. He would assume their guilt. He would take their punishment. He would die for His people. This also required that He became a flesh-and-blood man. It is not enough for God to appear as a man; He must *be* a man. It is not enough for God simply to bury the hatchet and forget our offenses; He must get us back.
- So He came into this world as a flesh-and-blood man—not having been conceived in the normal manner as the rest of us. Rather, He was conceived as the sinless Son of God yet with the nature of a man, which He received from His mother, Mary. And this God-man, whom we know as Jesus, carried out His plan. He lived and died for you and me. There is a wonderful hymn stanza that captures this:

    When from the dust of death I rise
    To claim my mansion in the skies,
    This then shall be my only plea:
    Jesus hath lived and died for me. (*LSB* 563:5)

- The motivation for this in the heart of God is pure love of us. He loved us the way you love your daughters, Lloyd. He is motivated only because He loves.

And that is the reason for the virgin birth. The virgin birth of Jesus is one of the first steps upon which Jesus embarked with the sole purpose of getting us back to Himself.

◇◇◇◇

The Verifiability and Falsifiability of Miracles

Letter 7

If a miracle is to have any credibility it must be both verifiable and falsifiable; it must be proved or disproved. Let's say there was some miracle worker on television who claimed that he could actually cure cancer simply by laying his hands on you. You could, with relative ease, either prove or disprove such a claim: Find someone with cancer. Have medical experts evaluate the patient. Then bring that person to the TV miracle worker and make sure that he lays his hands on the man to heal him. Bring the cancer patient back to the doctors and have them test him again. If he is cancer free, then you can find another cancer patient and follow the same process. If it works three or four times, I think you might be on to something. The claim of the miracle worker has been verified. If the patients are not healed, then the claims of the miracle worker have been falsified.

The trouble with virtually every self-proclaimed miracle worker is that they have built in a "cop-out" to their failures. They will claim that the patient does not have a strong enough faith, thereby blaming the patient for their own failures.

Jesus did not do that. He healed the centurion's son from a distance without ever ascertaining at all that the boy believed (Luke 7:1–10). Jesus raised at least three people from the dead—two of whom He had never met and of whom there is no indication that they believed either before or after their having been raised. I speak of the widow's son from Nain and of Jairus's daughter (Luke 7:11–17; 8:49–56). Jesus did not depend on the faith of the person on whom He worked a miracle.

True, there are cases where Jesus worked a miracle in response to faith, such as the healing of the daughter of the Canaanite woman (Matthew 15:21–28) or the men who brought their paralyzed friend to Jesus and actually tore off the roof of a house to get their friend in front of Jesus (Mark 2:1–12). But these stories never make it seem as though faith is a prerequisite. Rather, faith is indicated, and Jesus responds. In many cases faith is not indicated, and Jesus still responds.

The miracles of Jesus are not only verifiable; they are presented to show that Jesus wants people to attempt to verify His claims of a miracle. He is open to testing. A good example is when Jesus healed the official's son (John 4:46–54). A man came to Jesus and asked for his son to be healed. Jesus told him to go home and assured him that the son would live. The man returned home eager to see his son. On the way he met some servants who told him that the son had recovered. They seemed unaware of the conversation the official had had with Jesus. The official then asked his servants to tell him the exact hour that the fever lifted. He discovered that it was precisely when Jesus spoke the words.

The writer of the miracle story, John, is willing to admit that there might be an alternate explanation to the fever lifting. Maybe the kid just got better. Maybe some other doctor showed up at the house. So he adds this little detail of the healing occurring "at the seventh hour . . . when Jesus had said to him, 'Your son will live' " (John 4:52–53). Now Lloyd, even if you do not believe the miracle of Jesus healing the official's son, you must certainly recognize that the Bible writers understood the importance of subjecting their claims of miracles to tests of verifiability. This is especially the case with the resurrection of Jesus from the tomb, which I will tell you about soon.

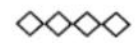

Satisfying the Skeptics

Letter 8

Miracles need to convince skeptics. If a miracle is convincing only to someone who is gullible or predisposed to faith, then there will be no serious attempts at falsifying the miracle. That would make the miracle story suspicious. Miracles must be tested if they are to be believed. The healing of the blind man is a great example of Jesus working a miracle that is then investigated by skeptics.

Jesus heals "a man blind from birth" and immediately people set out to falsify the miracle. Some suggest that it is a case of mistaken identity. This seeing man, they claim, is not the same person who was born blind. "He just looks like him." But the man asserts, "I am the man" (John 9:9). So the mistaken identity theory is disproved, and the miracle, apparently, stands.

But the skeptics are not satisfied. They think that the man is too young or incompetent to understand these things. They send for the man's parents and demand to know if this is their son, if he was truly born blind, and how this happened. "We know this is our son and that he was born blind. But how he now sees we do not know, nor do we know who opened his eyes. Ask him; he is of age. He will speak for himself" (John 9:20–21). So the second test of the skeptics is answered. The man is capable of analyzing these things accurately.

They try a third strategy to discount the miracle. They conclude that because the man had been told to carry his bed on the Sabbath, and this was against the Jewish law, this must mean that the miracle worker (Jesus) was a sinner and ungodly. "We know that God has spoken to Moses, but as for this man, we do not know where He comes from" (John 9:29). Notice that this is not an attempt to falsify the miracle as much as it is to discredit the one who performed the miracle. At any rate, the blind man turns the tables on them. "If this man were not from God, He could do nothing" (John 9:33). At that the Jewish leaders threw him out of the temple.

Observe that the skeptics unsuccessfully tried to prove the miracle. True miracle workers are simply unafraid to have their miracles tested. Jesus is a true miracle worker, and He was unafraid.

Now someone may say that they will not believe in biblical miracles because these miracles were not subjected to the most rigorous tests. Now skeptics claim that if Jesus' miracles were performed today, then our new scientific tests would have a better chance to falsify the miracle. But that is true only if the miracle is false. The fact is that the miracles were subjected to all the tests that were available to the people of that day. And what more tests than these could be applied to miracles? If you disbelieve miracles simply because today's science is not applied to them, you are making it impossible to verify any past.

Let's say that God did miracles today and no one could falsify the miracles. Don't you suppose that five hundred years from now someone would complain that his or her science could prove the miracle wrong? Obviously there will be advances in science in the next five hundred years. And if God waited five hundred years from now to do a miracle, then people five hundred years after that would complain. With this way of thinking, God would have to do miracles in just about every generation in order to allow these miracles to be subjected to falsifying tests. But, as I showed earlier, miracles must be relatively rare to be at all meaningful. And since God's plan was to come into this world *once* to intervene for us, then God's plan was to offer a bunch of miracles at that one time. Jesus had to come at some point in time. He couldn't keep waiting to come just because He knew that a few hundred years afterwards people would doubt His miracles since their modern science is more advanced than the science of Jesus' day. The moment Christ made a commitment to come at a certain time He was making it possible for all people of subsequent times to insist that miracles must be tested by them in order to be believed. But this is an expectation that, if fulfilled, would completely destroy the whole purpose for a miracle in the first place.

The Challenge of the Virgin Birth

Letter 9

Of all the miracles in the New Testament, it strikes me that the story of the virgin birth of Jesus is the most difficult to verify or to falsify, making it an easy target for skeptics.

Most miracles are done before crowds, providing all sorts of witnesses. But the angel appeared to Mary while she was alone. Further, immediately after the report of a miracle you can disprove or prove it. But this is extremely difficult with the virgin birth. We may actually be able to explain some of those miraculous events.

Now I speak as an unbelieving skeptic, Lloyd, but I trust that God will forgive me if I can convince you. Let's say that the Bible is false, and that you shouldn't necessarily believe it just because it says so. What if we can come up with an alternate theory of the birth of Jesus? Let's hypothesize that Joseph and Mary had an affair and didn't want to expose themselves to the public humiliation of a pregnancy in the small town of Nazareth. Joseph, aware of the census that had been ordered by Caesar Augustus, had a hasty wedding and decided to travel to Bethlehem for his child's birth. An innkeeper, seeing the young family camped out in the town square, had compassion on the family and offered them a place to stay. Eventually, Joseph fled to Egypt and returned to Bethlehem a couple of years later with toddler and wife in tow. No one would be the wiser regarding the timing of the little boy's birth relative to the wedding. Perhaps Mary made up the story of the angel announcing the birth of Jesus. Let's say that when Jesus became famous, she embellished the events of His birth to give His popularity a boost.

Now that's an alternate theory which does, I believe, take into consideration most or all of the data from the Bible. It is certainly more plausible to our human understanding, especially if you don't believe in miracles. But there are a couple of problems with this alternate story. First, there is no evidence from any eyewitness or anyone close to the story that my version is actually what happened. We can theorize two thousand years later that this story makes more sense, but that doesn't make it true. In fact, if we were honest, we would have to admit that the only reason anyone would believe this alternate explanation of the facts is to explain away the story of the miracle. People just don't want to believe in the virgin birth. There is, frankly, an anti-miracle bias that forces people to accept alternate explanations.

There is a second, more formidable flaw with the theory that Joseph is the biological father of the child. Was Jesus really so popular as to necessitate His mother making up a story about His birth? Actually, Jesus' popularity had seriously waned in the days leading up to His death. In John 6 it is reported that most of His disciples had left Him. And don't forget that when He was crucified, it is reported that all His disciples ran away—one was even naked. He was certainly not popular while hanging on the cross. Matthew wrote his Gospel around AD 50; and Luke in about AD 55–60. These two obviously believed that Jesus was born of a virgin. What happened between the year AD 30 and the year AD 55 to make them believe this of Jesus? How did a crucified prophet get so popular that His disciples would believe such an amazing claim? It would require an event more profoundly miraculous and inexplicable by natural standards than the virgin birth itself. It would require the resurrection of Jesus from the grave.

◇◇◇◇

The Resurrection of Christ

Letter 10

It seems to me that the only way you can explain the virgin birth story, unverifiable and unfalsifiable as it is, is if Jesus rose from the dead. And if you can believe that Jesus miraculously rose from the dead, then you can certainly believe that He was miraculously born of a virgin. The story of the resurrection, after the story of the crucifixion, is the central story of the Bible. It is attested to by all four Gospels and by almost every Epistle. If the resurrection is historically true, then the claims of Christianity are true. If the resurrection can be proven false, then Christianity is the greatest hoax in the history of the world. Further, if Jesus did not rise from the dead, then Jesus is the greatest deceiver and fraud we could imagine.

Before we analyze the historical truth of the resurrection let's understand what is at stake in the discussion. Paul very clearly in 1 Corinthians 15:1–22 spells out what the resurrection means to the world and to you, Lloyd. If Jesus has not risen from the dead, then there are four other truths we must face: First, if Jesus did not rise from the dead, then any preaching or teaching of Christ is worthless. Second, if Christ did not rise from the dead, then faith in Him is futile. Third, if Christ did not rise from the dead, then the apostles and writers of the Bible are a bunch of liars.

All this must be obvious to anyone. The Christian Church has been proclaiming a risen Lord for two thousand years. Based on that resurrection we have said that faith is precious, preaching is powerful, and the Bible is true. If Jesus is in some earthly grave near Jerusalem, then He is a pathetic man whose followers are evil geniuses. If Jesus did not rise, the apostles took a dead guy and made something of Him by creating a lie.

If Jesus is still dead, then such a lie has deceived millions over the years. If Jesus is still dead, then I, as a pastor, have wasted my life and Jan, as a teacher of young Christians, has wasted hers as well. If Jesus is still dead, then your daughters, who place their confidence in Him, are deluded. A lot is at stake in the discussion.

But especially, Lloyd, "If Christ has not been raised . . . then those also who have fallen asleep in Christ have perished. If in Christ we have hope in this life only, we are of all people most to be pitied" (1 Corinthians 15:17–18). So says Paul. That's the fourth truth implicit in the resurrection.

When you die, Lloyd, what will happen? If Jesus has not risen, then when you die, you are lost whether you believe in Him or not. I suppose that you can comfort yourself with the belief that after death there is neither heaven nor hell but only nothingness. And that is certainly more comforting than believing that there is a hell. But beliefs are pretty irrelevant here. What matters is not what you or I believe. What matters is what's true. What is the truth? If Jesus rose from the dead, then what He said and did is true and valid for all people and for all times and, specifically, Lloyd, for you. If Jesus rose from the dead, then, in Him, you also will rise.

There is so much at stake in the discussion of this miracle that the Bible writers go to great lengths to show that the story of the resurrection of Jesus from the grave on the third day is really the only possible explanation of the facts. The resurrection is true not because many people wish it to be true. It is true not just because we can't face life without it. It is true not just because we have never given thought to another possibility. It is true not just because lots of people, myself included, believe it. The resurrection is true because it happened.

Lloyd began to improve within a few days of my initial conversation with him, though his condition was still critical. I had written the first nine letters within the first week of being home while Jan, my wife, stayed with her father and sisters back in Fresno. By the time she rejoined me in Minnesota I was up at the summer cabin and Lloyd had recovered remarkably. So I interrupted the flow of my writings with a happy letter of congratulations. When you are talking to family about Jesus, you sometimes have to interrupt yourself and let them set the agenda for the conversation.

Miracle Recovery?

Letter 11

As Jan has told you, Lloyd, we had a wonderful time with the kids and extended family up at the lake last week. One night, we toasted you as Jan gave us the news that the reports of your imminent demise were, as Mark Twain once said, greatly exaggerated. I cannot tell you how happy this makes me to hear that you are gaining some weight, exercising more, and even possibly reading a bit. I know how much you love to read. I pray that you can even make it to your computer and read these little thoughts of mine for yourself without having to rely on others to do so.

I would be tempted, Lloyd, to call your improvement a miracle. There is no doubt that your improvement falls upon the immediate heels of many prayers that have ascended to God from the lips of those who love you. Clearly all your daughters as well as your grandchildren and their loved ones have consistently prayed for you. We mention you in our Sunday prayers every week and also on Monday evenings. I am aware of many members who have placed you in their private prayers as well. So, it seems that God has intervened on your behalf.

But I have defined a miracle as when God breaks or defies the normal laws of nature. And, while I do thank God for your improvement, I do not think that God has defied the laws of nature to do so. Don't worry Lloyd, this doesn't mean that I will cease my prayers on your behalf. God does many things through natural means. I have four lovely children, all gifts of God for which I thank Him daily, but these kids are not miracles. God daily provides me with food and warmth, but these are not miracles. God has provided me with a wonderful wife, as you yourself know since you gave me her hand in marriage, but even that is not a miracle.

Your recuperation is, however, an act of God within the laws of nature. And Lloyd, while I do not know what God's intent might be in prolonging your life, I cannot help but think that maybe this will give me a chance to write to you about the actions of God in Christ that are, indeed, miraculous. I am hopeful that this time might afford me the chance to come again to visit you before the end of the year as I promised.

The resurrection of Jesus from the grave is a miracle—one that many have questioned or denied. I provided an alternate explanation for the virgin birth of Christ, which was, perhaps, plausible—assuming the Bible is not true. Let me now present some of the alternate explanations of the empty grave that have been propounded. I will show that none of these explanations is at all reasonable. There is only one way to explain the remarkable events that transpired in that corner of the world those many years ago. Jesus rose from the dead.

My desire to write to Lloyd was interrupted by the arrival of a letter from him that contained six questions. Lloyd's questions suggested that he believed some of the "Time/Warner" theology as I labeled it. This is theology that you get from popular, shallow, and non-Christian magazines or TV shows. Lloyd wondered why Jesus was mentioned only in the Bible and not other writings. He thought that the New Testament documents weren't written until the third century. He thought that Jesus never made any claims for divinity Himself but that the Church manufactured these claims in the third century.

So, despite my eagerness to move the conversation to a discussion of the implications of the cross, I had to write letters twelve and thirteen to answer Lloyd's questions, even though they interrupted the flow of my presentation. I am convinced that Lloyd would not have paid much attention to the discussion about the resurrection if I had not taken the time and effort to answer his questions.

◇◇◇◇

The First Witnesses

Letter 12

Before I write about the evidence of Christ's resurrection, let me say a couple things about the Bible and other first-century writings, especially since I have just now received the questions that you sent to Jan. A couple of those questions wondered about the date of the New Testament and other writings of the time.

The New Testament writers all wrote before the end of the first century. Matthew was written about AD 50. Mark was written a couple of years later. Luke was written about AD 55–60. John wrote his Gospel about AD 90. He is called "the elder" because he would have been pretty old, perhaps as old as you, Lloyd, when he penned his Gospel. Matthew and John are eyewitnesses of the events; John makes very strong claims to that effect twice. In John 19:35, immediately after he recounts the story of the piercing of Jesus' side, he says, "He who saw it has born witness—his testimony is true, and he knows that he is telling the truth—that you also may believe." Then in John 21:24 he says, "This is the disciple who is bearing witness about these things, and who has written these things, and we know that his testimony is true." John also writes in his first epistle, "That which was from the beginning, which we have heard, which we have seen with our eyes, which we looked upon and have touched with our hands, concerning the word of life" (1 John 1:1). Luke opens his Gospel with words that indicate that he knows the importance of painstaking research and accurate reporting. "Inasmuch as many have undertaken to compile a narrative of the things that have been accomplished among us, just as those who from the beginning were eyewitnesses and ministers of the Word have delivered them to us, it seemed good to me also, having followed all things closely for some time past, to write an orderly account for you, most excellent Theophilus, that you may have certainty concerning the things you have been taught" (Luke 1:1–4). The authors of the Gospels claim either to be eyewitnesses or to have interviewed them.

We can determine the dates of the writings by the following facts: Luke wrote both the Gospel bearing his name as well as the Book of Acts. Paul was executed in Rome about AD 68. Yet Luke, who meticulously recounts the actions of Paul, does not mention his death. This has led most Bible scholars to conclude that the Book of Acts was written before Paul died—sometime around AD 60–62. In Acts 1:1–2, Luke says, "In the first book, O Theophilus, I have dealt with all that Jesus began to do and teach until the day when He was taken up" to heaven. So we know that the Book of Luke was written before the Book of Acts. Further, even the detractors of the Gospel account concede that Luke seems to have borrowed certain material from Matthew and Mark. So the books of Matthew and Mark must have been written and must have enjoyed some circulation before the Book of Luke was written.

You asked why there was nothing written about Christ's life until hundreds of years later. The fact is that all twenty-seven writings of the New Testament were written much earlier than that. Until recently, all scholars accepted the conventional wisdom that the New Testament was written early in the New Testament era. Only lately has that been questioned; some so-called Bible "scholars" claim that the Gospels were written hundreds of years after Christ. You might even hear such claims on television documentaries. However, except for the writings of John, all of the New Testament writings came about within thirty-five years of the death of Jesus.

◇◇◇◇

Who Else Tells Us about Jesus?

 Letter 13

There are other books of the first century, besides the Bible, which make reference to the life and death of Jesus. Toward the end of the first century, Flavius Josephus, a Jewish historian, wrote the following:

> Now, there was about this time, Jesus, a wise man, if it be lawful to call him a man, for he was a doer of wonderful works, a teacher of such men as receive the truth with pleasure. He drew over to him both many of the Jews, and many of the Gentiles. He was the Christ, and when Pilate, at the suggestion of the principal men among us, had condemned him to the cross, those that loved him at the first did not forsake him; for he appeared to them alive again the third day; as the divine prophets had foretold these and ten thousand other wonderful things concerning him. And the tribe of Christians, so named from him, are not extinct at this day.[1]

Satirist Lucian spoke of Christians in the second century as worshiping Christ:

> Moreover their first lawgiver persuaded them that all of them might be brethren to each other, when, once for all, first having made transgression against the Greek gods, they utterly deny them; then, when they worship that crucified street-teacher of theirs and live according to his laws.[2]

Historian Cornelius Tacitus wrote in the early second century AD and recounted how Emperor Nero had blamed and punished the Christians for burning Rome. "Christ, the originator of the name [Christians], was executed by Pontius Pilate, procurator under Tiberius: but the deadly superstition, repressed for the present, broke out again—not only through Judea, where the evil originated, but through the City [Rome] as well."[3]

The writings of the New Testament must have been written shortly after the time of Christ in order for others to make reference to the claims of these writings. Tacitus and Lucian both wrote at about the turn of the century (AD 100). Josephus actually wrote a few years before that. Yet all three of these men knew about the claims of the Christians. Josephus seems to have believed the claims of the Christians while Tacitus and Lucian do not. But all three knew the claims. They knew that Jesus had been crucified under Pontius Pilate, that Christians claimed that Jesus rose, and that His followers worshiped Him and had abandoned the worship of the Greek gods. Whether this Jesus was a wise man or the author of pernicious superstition is not the question here. Rather, the question is the date of the writings. For men to have written either in contempt of the Christian religion or in defense of it, the Christian religion must have already existed. But for the Christian religion to have existed there must have been some record of the events that Christians claimed were the historical basis of their religion. So the writings of Christians—in other words, the New Testament—must have been written before the end of the first century.

These New Testament writings must have been fairly popular for others to comment about them. And this is a testimony to the fact that they were written early after Jesus' death. Generally, people don't write against things that aren't threatening. If the memory of Jesus had simply faded into memory, then there would have been no need to speak against the religion. In my ministry I don't regularly warn people of Jim Jones and the "People's Temple." Remember him? He was the guy who manipulated nine hundred people to drink poisoned Kool-Aid after having enticed them to move to South America. But that religion is dead and gone. I don't regularly warn people about the Christian Scientist religion since it is all but dead. Why warn people of something that poses no threat? But I would certainly warn against Scientology or other cults that have an attraction for many today, and even have the capacity to entice Christians away from the faith. I do take the time to inform my people of the claims of Islam and Mormonism. That's because both Islam and Mormonism are formidable world religions that oppose Christianity. In the first century the detractors of Christianity warned against it. That means that Christianity must have been a fairly well-established religion by the end of the first century. That could not have happened unless the writings of the Christians had been written early and had been taught for a number of years.

Jesus was believed to be God from the very beginnings of the Christian religion. Lucian says that His followers were "worshiping the crucified street-teacher." You don't worship someone unless you believe that He is God. Another writer of the first century, Pliny the Younger (governor of Bithynia in Asia Minor), wrote in the first decade of the second century wondering how best to deal with Christians. He says he made attempts that the Christians "would curse Christ, none of which those who are true Christians can be compelled to do."[4] Pliny the Younger also complained of the Christians: "They affirmed this to have been the totatlity of their fault or error: that they were accustomed to convene on a set date before light, and to sing responsively a hymn to Christ as to a god, and to pledge themselves not to some villainy, but to commit neither theft nor banditry nor adultery, nor to cheat a trust, nor to refuse a trust when called."[5] So, late in the first century, their detractors were complaining that Christians were treating Christ as God.

The Council of Nicaea (late third or fourth century) was not the first time Jesus was recognized and honored as God. He was believed to be God immediately—during His own time. Jesus Himself claimed to be God, which I will explain in a future letter. During the first century thousands of Christians lost their lives at the hands of Trajan, Nero, and other tyrannical emperors. The reason Christians were martyred is not because they made certain benign and innocuous claims about Jesus. They were martyred because they worshiped Jesus as their Lord and their God.

Why would they be willing to die for Jesus? This can only be explained by His resurrection.

◇◇◇◇

Was the Grave Empty?

Letter 14

Miracles must be verifiable or falsifiable. There must be some way to prove or disprove a miracle. That is why the virgin birth is somewhat challenging to prove or disprove. The resurrection, however, is one of the easiest claims to falsify.

Let's imagine that you are a Jewish leader on the Sunday after the crucifixion. You have been largely responsible, at least humanly speaking, for the charges against Jesus and His subsequent execution. You are pleased and relieved that He is dead because you think that He was a fraud who was misleading the people. But then you begin to hear rumors that He has been raised from the dead. The apostles are making noise. Reports from certain women are trickling back to you. Some of the other Jewish leaders are acting as though they might actually believe Jesus. You are beginning to be a bit alarmed at this unexpected turn of events. What would you do?

Well, I would appeal to Pilate to have the body exhumed to see for my own eyes that Jesus was dead. I would place the body uncovered on a platform in the middle of the city. Better yet, I would parade the body around the city with the announcement that Jesus of Nazareth most certainly is and remains dead.

All of Jerusalem had witnessed the preaching of Jesus. Most had seen His trial, and many had observed both the bearing of the cross and the crucifixion itself. All would have recognized Jesus. The Jewish leaders would have had an easy and final way to falsify the resurrection: produce the dead body. That would have ended the attempts of Christ and His followers once and for good. The Christian religion, which is based on the historical fact of the resurrection, would never have begun.

To me, the only reasonable conclusion that can be drawn from the fact that His detractors did not produce the dead body of Jesus is that they had no access to it. It was gone. And the disciples certainly did not steal the body. So what happened to it? Was it replaced? Hardly. The inevitable conclusion, and this is the claim of the witnesses closest to the events, is that, amazing as it may seem, Jesus actually rose from the dead.

If it is impossible for a miracle to happen, then, of course, you have to explain the missing body in some other way. And I will talk about these other ways in the next few days. For today, Lloyd, simply try to conceive of an explanation for the Jews' inability to show the dead corpse. The only explanation is that they could not. Given their motivation, the Jews' inability to produce the dead body is a very strong testimony to an empty grave.

WHERE DID THE BODY GO?

Letter 15

Jesus' tomb was empty. How did it get that way? One of the earliest explanations of the empty grave is that the disciples stole the body. In fact, the evangelist Matthew claims that this theory of the empty grave was made up by the Jewish leaders in an attempt to debunk the claims of the early Christian Church. The Pharisees went to Pilate and said, "We remember how that imposter said, while He was still alive, 'After three days I will rise.' Therefore order the tomb to be made secure until the third day, lest His disciples go and steal Him away and tell the people, 'He has risen from the dead,' . . . Pilate said to them, 'You have a guard of soldiers. Go, make it as secure as you can' " (Matthew 27:63–65). Later, after it was reported that Jesus had been raised, Matthew maintains that the guards went to the Pharisees who "gave a sufficient sum of money to the soldiers and said, 'Tell people, "His disciples came by night and stole Him away while we were asleep" ' " (Matthew 28:13).

Noteworthy in Matthew's report is the fact that both sides in the disagreement claim not to have the body. The Christians, of course, claim that Jesus was raised from the dead. The Pharisees claim that the Christians stole the body. Both agree that the body is gone and cannot be accounted for. Noteworthy also is that the earliest of Christian writers were making some efforts to defend the Christian message against the claims of a stolen body. So the Christians knew how devastating it would be to their message and their religion should people believe that the body was stolen.

How reasonable is it to believe that the apostles stole the body of Jesus? Not very, and here's why. One of the chief objections to the stolen body theory is that the disciples would not have been able to pull it off. Remember that Pilate had placed a guard around the tomb, probably sixteen men, according to historians. These guards would sleep in eight-man shifts. For the disciples to steal the body, they would have had to overpower sixteen armed guards. This seems quite unlikely.

Some have suggested that all sixteen of the guards fell asleep. This theory would hold that the disciples quietly stepped over all the sleeping men, broke the seal that the governor had placed on the grave, rolled away a huge stone, carried out a corpse, and disappeared into the night—all without disturbing even one of the men. It also holds that all sixteen men had fallen asleep at the same time, even though they had, no doubt, been warned that there might be a grave robbery attempt.

Now, Lloyd, imagine that you are one of the eight guards whose turn it is to stay awake. And imagine that one by one your comrades are falling asleep at the watch, even though they have been warned of grave robbers. And you know if you all fall asleep and some mischief does occur, then you are going to be in some serious trouble. How many of your fellow guards would you allow to sleep on the job before you started to wake them up?

Some have suggested that the disciples burrowed into the grave from the other side. Back then the graves were often dug in the side of hills, so I suppose that it would have been possible to tunnel through the hill into the tomb of Jesus and take the body while the guards were all expecting a frontal assault. But this theory assumes that the disciples could dig all night with clanging spades or shovels in such a way as not to arouse the suspicion of the guards. It also assumes that the grave was built into a hill made primarily of dirt. Matthew makes the claim that Jesus' body was placed into a tomb cut out of stone (Matthew 27:60), making the task virtually impossible.

Now, Lloyd, I know that many people are quite skeptical about the truth of the Bible. But we do know that Jesus died. We do know that they couldn't produce the body. It seems unlikely that the disciples could possibly have stolen the body either by force or by stealth. There is, further, one more reason, even stronger than the ones mentioned, to question the stolen body theory. But that will have to wait until tomorrow.

◇◇◇◇

Why Steal Jesus' Body?

Letter 16

What motivation would the disciples have to steal the body of Jesus?

For me to believe that the disciples stole the body of Jesus I would have to believe the following:

- Men who were so cowardly that they all ran away when their best friend still had a chance of being rescued suddenly got so bold and courageous that they were willing to risk their lives just to create a lie about Him.
- These same men dedicated their own lives to spreading the message of the resurrection of Jesus even though they all knew that it was a lie.
- These same men were completely willing to die for this lie that they themselves had created.

According to church tradition, all of the apostles except John were martyred for their confession. Now, martyrdom is nothing new for people of faith. History is full of dramatic stories of people who died rather than deny Jesus—from Polycarp to Jan Hus, from St. Stephen (Acts 7) to the young girl at Columbine who was shot by the deranged young man who told her he would kill her if she did not deny her Lord. I would like to believe that I would never deny Jesus even at the pain of death. Martyrs are admirable, but not if they are liars.

Think about the apostles stealing the body of Jesus. If that is the case, then they were killed for something they knew was a lie. Would twelve men all die for the same lie? That seems so unlikely as to be completely impossible. Yet that is what we have to believe if we hold that the disciples stole the body of Jesus.

The grave was empty and the disciples were not responsible for its emptiness. So is there another explanation?

◇◇◇◇

Was the Body Misplaced?

Letter 17

It's true that on occasion a body is misplaced. Sometimes bodies are misidentified. But it seems wholly unlikely that such was the case with Jesus.

First of all, the account of Matthew is written in such a way as to anticipate and discount precisely this alternate explanation of the empty tomb. Back then they did not bury people underground, as is our custom. Instead, people were usually placed into a tomb, which was essentially a cave cut into the side of a hill. These caves often had shelves cut into the walls or built upon the floor that could accommodate any number of bodies. A corpse would be embalmed and wrapped in linen that had been treated with fluid, which subsequently hardened. This way the body was almost literally wrapped in a cast. There could be a dozen or so bodies in a single family tomb. Obviously, it would be very easy to get the bodies confused in this procedure, especially because you would open the tomb only when another burial was necessary. So confusion of bodies was a real possibility.

Joseph of Arimathea was of the Jewish ruling council and one of only a couple of men on the council who actually was willing to listen to the claims of the Messiah. He offered his tomb to hold Jesus' body. "Joseph took the body and wrapped it in a clean linen shroud and laid it in his own new tomb" (Matthew 27:59–60). Notice the mention that the tomb is *new*. This would mean that there were no other bodies in the tomb. It would not be possible to confuse the body with another. There was only one body in the grave on Friday night and no bodies on Sunday morning.

But perhaps the body was confused with another before it was placed into the grave. This seems unlikely unless one would think that Joseph purposely hid the body somewhere else and subsequently lied about the body being in the grave. This theory places the deception upon Joseph rather than the twelve and so it does not have the conspiratorial tone of the previous theories. However, the Gospel of John tells us that Nicodemus helped Joseph, and Luke tells us that the women who followed Jesus witnessed the whole thing. So if Joseph had attempted deception it would not be without witnesses. And you still have the difficulty of understanding why Joseph would lie.

Well, maybe it wasn't a lie but a simple mistake. Perhaps they just picked up the wrong body among several bodies being prepared for burial. This still doesn't solve the problem because it suggests that some other person died at precisely the same time and then that person's body was raised from the dead. Then you have a resurrection of a total stranger.

In all this it seems quite apparent that the body was neither stolen nor mistaken nor misplaced. Yet the empty grave must somehow be explained.

There is one more theory that I will mention tomorrow: the Swoon Theory.

◇◇◇◇

Did Jesus Really Die?

Letter 18

One of the more intriguing attempts to explain the empty tomb without accepting the resurrection of Christ is called the Swoon Theory. This theory holds that Jesus never died. What happened, it is claimed, is that Jesus just appeared to die—He swooned.

Typically, crucifixion causes asphyxiation. Someone who is crucified would be nailed or tied to the cross and gradually lose the ability to hold himself upright. Once he leaned forward, he would be unable to breathe. So, he would hoist himself back up, hold himself erect, and commence breathing again. Then the cycle would start over. The end result was that, exhausted from exposure, dehydration, bleeding, and sleeplessness, the crucified person would inevitably lose the ability to hold himself erect and would die. Sometimes the process would take days. Sometimes, if the officials wanted to hasten the process, they would break the legs of the crucified. Then the man on the cross would slump over and, unable to breathe, die quickly. It was actually a merciful thing to do, given the circumstances.

Jesus hung on the cross a mere six hours, next to two crucified criminals (Mark 15:25–37). When Friday evening approached, it occurred to the Jews who were responsible that they did not want the bodies on the grave past sundown because the Jewish Sabbath always began on Friday evening and ended Saturday evening. To hasten death, the soldiers were told to break the bones of the three men on the crosses. According to the Book of John, the soldiers found that Jesus was already dead, so they did not break His bones (19:33).

The swoon theory says that Jesus simply did not have enough time to die in a scant six hours. Further, this theory holds that the soldiers made a mistake by not breaking His bones and by taking Him down off the cross too early. Subsequently Jesus, who had been wrapped in clothes and buried, came out of His state of unconsciousness and escaped from the grave.

I hope you can see how difficult it is to believe this theory. It requires us to believe that the soldiers just happened to make a mistake on the one man who predicted that He would rise. It seems to me that they would have taken special pains to make sure that Jesus, of all people, was dead. This theory also requires us to believe that Joseph of Arimathea, the man who placed Jesus in the tomb, did not see that He was breathing and alive. It also holds that Jesus gained consciousness in the grave, mustered up enough strength to break out of the tightly-wrapped linen clothes, and rolled away the stone at the entrance of the tomb—all without disturbing the guards. Finally, this theory holds that Jesus appeared to His disciples that very evening and instilled such confidence in them that immediately they went out and began preaching. It seems more likely, if He was merely a man who had swooned, that Jesus would have sought medical help instead of meeting with His disciples.

This theory, and others, shows the lengths people will go to deny the resurrection. It is not the facts, the common sense, or the eyewitness accounts that make people skeptical. There is only one reason, ultimately, why people do not accept that Jesus rose from the dead: it is just too uncomfortable for them. It is a truth far too painful.

Why Don't People Believe?

Letter 19

In the previous weeks I have shown, Lloyd, that the grave of Jesus was empty and that the only reasonable explanation of that empty grave is that Jesus rose from the dead. Yet people do not often believe the accounts of the resurrection. Why not?

Some claim that they are being true skeptics. That is a fine posture to take, I believe, but there comes a time when skepticism must bow to the facts. Here are the facts: The eyewitnesses, and there were many, were utterly convinced of it. The earliest writings testify to the resurrection. There were plenty of opportunities to disprove it. Resurrections are easily falsifiable, as I have shown. The motivation to lie about it is simply not present. The ability to steal the body either by stealth or force is not there. Jesus must have risen from the dead. So why the reluctance to believe?

I am convinced that there is really one primary reason why people do not believe that Jesus rose from the dead: because it is too painful. Let me explain.

If Jesus rose from the dead, then He must be God. He claimed as much throughout His ministry (which I will write about next time). If He is God, then He has a claim on us. If He has a claim on us, then we do not belong to ourselves, but to Him. And human nature does not want to admit that we must answer to someone else. It's as simple as that.

A few weeks after the death and resurrection of Jesus, Peter was preaching a sermon. In it he told the people that they had unjustly killed Jesus. He concluded with this claim: "Let all the house of Israel therefore know for certain that God has made Him both Lord and Christ, this Jesus whom you crucified" (Acts 2:36). According to Peter, the resurrection of Jesus demonstrated that Jesus is our Lord and the promised Messiah.

The word *Lord* is the same word as the name of God in the Old Testament. (Again, I'll explain this in a future letter). The word *Christ* is the Greek word for the Hebrew word *Messiah*. Both words mean, in English, "Anointed One."

Remarkably, just a few days after his sermon, Peter was dragged before the Jewish court and told to cease and desist from his preaching. Why would these men try to silence Peter? Because they could not afford to admit that Jesus was Lord and Christ. For them to admit that Jesus was Lord would mean that He, not they, was really in charge of the Jewish nation; and not that nation only but all nations. They would have had to accept Jesus' commentary on their religion—and it wasn't particularly positive. For me to admit and concede that Jesus rose from the dead forces me also to admit that He is my Lord. And when I admit He is Lord, then my life belongs to Him, not to me anymore.

The historical fact of the resurrection is not and can never remain merely a historical fact. If Jesus was raised, then I owe Him my devotion, my allegiance, my loyalty, and everything I am and have. If He is Lord, then I must pray to Him and worship Him. If He is Lord, then I must rely on Him for my identity as a Christian and as a man. If He is Lord, then, as Paul says, "Every knee should bow, in heaven and on earth and under the earth, and every tongue confess that Jesus Christ is Lord, to the glory of God the Father" (Philippians 2:10–11). If He is Lord, then I must be willing to risk everything rather than offend or lose Him. If He is Lord, then I lose myself. I am no longer the master of my destiny. I am no longer the captain of my ship. If Jesus is Lord, then I must learn to rely on Him and not upon myself, my own heart, or my own understanding. That is scary. It is painful. It is one aspect of faith.

◇◇◇◇

Letter 20

Jesus was not called Lord for the first time only after His resurrection. Certainly, people knew much better that He was the Lord once they saw He had risen. Thomas confessed Christ when he saw and touched Jesus' wounds after His resurrection. "My Lord and my God!" were his words (John 20:28). But there are indications that Jesus was called Lord throughout His own lifetime.

One of the most familiar stories in the entire New Testament is the Christmas story from Luke 2. It tells of how the shepherds were watching their flocks when the entire heavenly host showed up with remarkable news: "For unto you is born this day in the city of David a Savior, who is Christ the Lord" (Luke 2:11). Notice that the same titles given to Him upon His resurrection were also placed upon Jesus when His birth was announced. He is Christ and Lord, though He hid who He was under the humanity and lowliness that He had assumed. But every once in a while it showed. Here are a couple of examples.

Matthew relates how Jesus was questioning the disciples about what people were saying about Him. They gave Him a couple of answers and then He turned things personal. "Who do you say that I am?" Simon Peter answered, "You are the Christ, the Son of the living God" (Matthew 16:16). Now, Lloyd, if Jesus did not claim to be God then, He certainly would have corrected Peter. Even Paul corrected those who thought he was a god (Acts 14:11–18). But Jesus, knowing who He was, answered Peter: "Flesh and blood has not revealed this to you, but My Father who is in heaven" (Matthew 16:17). He claimed to be the Son of God.

Luke tells the story of Jesus healing ten leprous men (17:11–18). Lepers were to live apart from all others due to their contagious disease. When Jesus healed the ten, He told them to go on their way to the priests who would give them a clean bill of health and allow them back into society. One of the men, a Samaritan, turned around and fell before Jesus (the Greek literally means bend the knee so as to worship). Jesus asked: “Was no one found to return and give praise to God except this foreigner?” Now I have to believe that the other nine had praised God for being healed. The one who bowed before Jesus, however, is identified as *returning* to praise God. Jesus is claiming to be God in a specific place and time.

When the high priests questioned Jesus (Matthew 26:62–65), they demanded, “Tell us if You are the Christ, the Son of God.” “You have said so,” Jesus replied, “But I tell you, from now on you will see the Son of Man sitting at the right hand of Power and coming on the clouds of heaven.” This is clearly a claim that He is the glorious Son of God, the Christ, who sits at the right hand of the “Mighty One.” In the Bible, the expression “sitting at the right hand” indicates equality. Jesus truly is the Christ, the Son of God, who sits at the right hand of the Father and will come again in glory.

Jesus' Claim to Have God's Name

Letter 21

Possibly the most extravagant claim of Jesus is recorded in John 8. The chapter contains a prolonged conversation between Jesus and His detractors concerning Jesus' relationship with His heavenly father, as well as His relationship with father Abraham. Jesus proclaimed, "Your father Abraham rejoiced that he would see My day. He saw it and was glad." At this point his Jewish opponents were incredulous. "You are not yet fifty years old," they exclaimed, "and have You seen Abraham?" Jesus replied, "Truly, truly, I say to you, before Abraham was, I am" (vv. 56–58).

This claim contains much more than immediately meets the eye. Let me explain.

Exodus 3 records a conversation between God and Moses. It's the famous story of God speaking through the burning bush. God wants Moses to lead His children to the freedom of the Promised Land, but Moses is reluctant. Who is he to lead God's nation? Suppose the people question him about this very conversation. Moses wants to know God's name. "God said to Moses, 'I AM WHO I AM.' And He said, 'Say this to the people of Israel, "I AM has sent me to you" ' " (3:14).

The name of God is "I AM." The Hebrew word from which comes the phrase "I AM" is *Yahweh*, the name of God. Some Christians will use the word "Jehovah," which is derived from the Hebrew word "Yahweh." In Hebrew there are no vowels, so the name of God is actually YHWH.

However, Jewish people would never use this particular word. They considered the name of God to be so holy that they wouldn't speak it out loud. When they read the Hebrew Scriptures and came to the word *Yahweh* they would substitute a synonym for it, the word *Adonai,* which is translated as "Lord." This is not so much the name of God but His title. He is Lord.

The New Testament was written in Greek. The word for Lord in Greek is *Kyrios*, yet another title for God. We get the expression *Kyrie Eleison* from this word, which means, "Lord, have mercy." The word *Lord* is usually a reference to God but is not precisely the use of His name. Rather it is the most dominant of the many titles that God has. When Jesus is called Lord, it is a strong assertion about His deity because He is given the title of God. Other titles would be "Creator," "Son of God," "Almighty," or "Mighty One." But there is an even stronger way to talk about God, and that is to use His name.

Back to John 8:58. There, Jesus is not content to simply use the title of God by saying, "I am the Lord" or "I am the mighty one of Israel." Instead, He takes the name of God. He says, "Before Abraham was, I am." Jesus assumes the name of God by using the forbidden word, I AM, to refer to Himself. He takes the names of God and places it upon Himself.

Notice the reaction of His opponents in John 8:59. They take up stones to kill Him! It is a capital offense to take upon yourself the name of God.

The same thing happens in Luke 22:70. Jesus is asked if He is the Son of God. His response is, "You say that I am." It's like He's saying, "You said so; I am." Again the reaction indicates the profundity of the claim. The Jews respond by killing Jesus. He has used the name of God for Himself.

Why is this important? Because the resurrection is not the first time that it occurred to people that Jesus is God. It is proof of His claims. There's a little "show and tell" going on in the Bible. First He tells us who He is, and then He shows us.

◇◇◇◇

Church Symbols

Letter 22

A common feature you might see in a church is a little figure of a dove, which is a symbol of the Holy Spirit. Some churches in Sweden have the dove hanging from the ceiling above the pulpit right over the head of the preacher as a reminder to the pastor that he is not standing there to inspire the people or to entertain them. Rather, he is to preach to them the Word of Jesus. Jesus said, [The Holy Spirit] "will glorify Me, for He will take what is Mine and declare it to you." So that is the pastor's job. The dove also reminds the people that when they listen to the pastor, they are also listening to God. So that little symbol serves an important function for both pastor and people.

When I was visiting Norway and Sweden, I noticed that in some of the churches the baptismal fonts were hundreds of years old. They were often made of stone. Consequently, when churches burnt down, as was not too uncommon, the fonts survived and were used in the new rebuilt churches. Or, if church buildings were replaced as congregations grew, the fonts always remained. These fonts are reminders to the people that the grace of God, which is given in Baptism, is possessed by one generation after the other as long as time endures. One font, it is said, has served thirty-two generations of Christian people.

I was also intrigued by little windows about three inches by six inches in the front of the church. They were typically cut right out of the wood and served no good purpose that I could see since they were too small for any appreciable light. I was told that the priest or pastor used them during Communion so that he could hand the Sacrament to the lepers who would be standing right outside of the church listening. I wondered if the pastors were ever afraid that they might catch the leprosy, and the answer was always the same: "No, it's their calling. Besides, the Lord's

Supper was too important to go without, and the pastors simply had to risk even death so that people could have it."

These unusual customs all stressed the manner in which God feeds our faith. It is not miracles that do so. Rather, God feeds our faith by the Word as it is proclaimed, by Baptism, and by the Lord's Supper. These are really what faith looks to and not to miracles, interesting though they are. I will write more on these in a few weeks.

Miracles and the Nature of Faith

Letter 23

In the Bible the miracles that Jesus performed were always impressive. The people were sometimes awestruck, sometimes fearful, sometimes intimidated, and even sometimes angry. But they were never unaffected by the miracles. Amazingly, however, miracles by themselves were inadequate to produce in people any kind of true faith in Jesus. Let me give a couple of examples.

On the Sabbath day, Jesus healed a blind man (John 9). After carefully questioning the man, the Jewish leaders could only conclude that a mighty act of God had occurred. Yet they were in no way ready to believe in Jesus as the Christ or as that one whom God had sent to redeem His people. Instead, they threw the man out of the synagogue. He was persecuted simply because he had confessed to believe in Jesus Christ. So a miracle produced unreasonable tyranny.

Jesus raised Lazarus from the dead as recorded in John 10. The response of His detractors was not to rejoice in the blessings of new life given to Lazarus. Nor was it to listen more attentively to Jesus. Instead, they plotted to kill Lazarus because his resurrection tended to make Jesus a bit more popular than they were.

Herod, the wicked king who ruled Judea at the time of Christ's birth, saw that a special star had been sent that the Wise Men followed. He saw that a prediction of the Old Testament had been fulfilled. And his response was to feign belief as a pretense of his plot to kill Jesus, as told in Matthew 2.

Jesus healed ten lepers according to Luke 17. But nine of them probably never saw Jesus again. They believed the miracle, but they went back to the lives they had before they had contracted the disease. They were unaffected by the miracle in any profound way. One of the ten whom Jesus healed came back, fell on his knees before Jesus, and actually believed in Him. Ten were healed, but only one believed. Miracles don't produce true faith. Even if I could convince you of every miracle that the Bible says, Lloyd, that would not mean that you truly believe in Jesus.

The belief in miracles is no guarantee of true faith or trust in Jesus. The opposite is often true. Sometimes witnessing miracles brought out the worst in people. Why? I think the same answer can be given that I gave to you a couple of letters ago. It's easy to believe in miracles, especially when they are staring you right in the face. But it is another thing altogether to believe in Jesus.

It is painful to believe in Jesus. When you believe in Jesus, it means that you have to admit that there is something outside of you far more important and significant than you are. Faith in Jesus means that you must admit that you need Him, that He gives you something you would otherwise never have. It means that you must depend on Him for certain blessings. What blessings?

Almost every worship service in the Lutheran Church begins in a certain way. The people either stand or kneel and say "Almighty God, merciful Father, I, a poor, miserable sinner, confess unto You all my sins and iniquities with which I have ever offended You and justly deserved Your temporal and eternal punishment. But I am heartily sorry for them and sincerely repent of them, and I pray You of Your boundless mercy and for the sake of the holy, innocent, bitter sufferings and death of Your beloved Son, Jesus Christ, to be gracious and merciful to me, a poor, sinful being" (*LSB*, p 184). That short confession of sins reflects the real reason for which Jesus came into the world. He came not to be a miracle worker but to forgive sins. So, to have faith in Jesus means more than an acceptance of His miracles. Faith means you have to admit that you have truly offended God and that Jesus is the only one who actually has forgiven you.

And it is not miracles that give us this forgiveness. Rather it is the lesson behind the miracles.

◇◇◇◇

Letter 24

Every miracle of Jesus proves that He is God. But each miracle also has a unique lesson to it, which points to Jesus and teaches us some aspect of the love He has toward us. They usually teach us about His crucifixion. I find learning the lessons of the miracles are enjoyable, challenging, and comforting.

There is a brief miracle told in Luke 6 of Jesus healing a man's withered hand on the Sabbath. Jesus' opponents were watching carefully to see if He would break the Sabbath law, which they understood to forbid Him doing a miracle on the Sabbath, even if it would heal someone. Now, Jesus could have waited a day to avoid the conflict. The man needing help was not near death. The whole purpose of the miracle, then, was not simply to help a poor unfortunate man. More than that, Jesus wanted to assert His authority over the Sabbath. He wanted to establish that He was a new Sabbath—a new opportunity for lasting rest. The old Sabbath was not needed.

According to Jewish thinking, God had established the Sabbath to protect people from working too hard or from forcing others to work too hard. That is not such a bad idea, but the Jewish religious leaders of Jesus' day had corrupted the Sabbath laws to the point of using them to oppress people rather than to serve people.

Jesus understood the real reason for the Jewish Sabbath law. It was so the people of God would understand that the blessings of God come to us without any work or effort on our part. Jesus says, "Come to Me, all who labor and are heavy laden, and I will give you rest" (Matthew 11:28). He is obviously not talking about physical rest on a specific day of the week. And He is not talking only about our eternal rest in heaven. He is talking about the tendency people have to think that they have to do a number of good deeds and exert themselves with certain spiritual work before they can come before God. Jesus is saying that we can come to God and expect to be accepted by Him simply through faith.

So this miracle recorded in Luke 6 teaches us that Jesus accepts us no matter how little we have worked because He loves us and died for us. We please God through Jesus, not through our work. Christians trust in Jesus, who gives us rest by doing everything for us. Christians trust they are pleasing to God because of Jesus.

This applies to everyone, Lloyd, including you. Jesus does not want you to believe in Him only after you are convinced that you have everything all worked out. He does not want you to wait until every skeptical doubt about miracles is gone from your head. He does not want you to be confident that you have done okay with your life. He simply wants you to recognize that you must be tired. He wants you to see that no matter how much good you have done in this world, it does not equal a saving faith in Christ. He wants tired people to trust that He has done everything for us. Take it easy. Have a rest. Jesus has done it all.

The Miracles of Touching

Letter 25

In Mark 5:21–43 there are two miracles that, while they may appear different at first, teach us the same unique and comforting lesson.

Jesus is called to the home of a synagogue ruler named Jairus, who pleads for Jesus to come and heal his dying daughter. On his way to Jairus's home, a crowd forms around Him. A woman touches Jesus' garment and is healed from a twelve-year uterine hemorrhage. Jesus announces that the woman's faith has healed her. Moving on to the home of Jairus, Jesus discovers that the little girl has just died. But instead of leaving, He goes to her room and takes her by the hand. "Little girl, I say to you, arise," He commands, and the little girl stands up.

In both miracles Jesus touches something unclean in order to heal. According to the Old Testament Book of Leviticus, which listed Jewish laws, when a woman was having her menstrual period, she was considered "unclean." If you touched such a woman, you were also unclean and had to go through a cleansing ritual. Likewise, the dead were unclean. Anyone touching a corpse was considered unclean. In both miracles listed in Mark 5, Jesus was willing to become unclean for the sake of others. He risked uncleanness for both the old woman and the young woman, and in both cases His willingness to be unclean was occasion for others to become clean.

No more is the old woman unclean, even though she had been bleeding for twelve years. No longer will the little girl be unclean, even though she had died. Instead, Jesus is unclean in their place.

The lesson for us is this: we are unclean before God because of who we are and what we do. We tend to downplay this in our thinking, especially if we have led fairly moral lives and not committed any terrible crimes. But we have to compare ourselves to the holiness and purity of God and evaluate ourselves by the perfect standards of the Almighty. And by these standards we are anything but clean, as I'm sure you would acknowledge.

How wonderful it is to know that Jesus has absorbed all of our impurities and uncleanness. When He went to the cross, He was the dirtiest man that ever lived because He had absorbed the sinful dirt and grime of countless unclean people, such as you and me. His crucifixion is the result of the impurities of you and me and the entire world. And His crucifixion cleansed those impurities. In Jesus we can stand before God as pure and spotless, because the pure and spotless Christ has absorbed our guilt.

The Miracle of Forgiveness

Letter 26

Possibly one of the most significant miracles Jesus performed is when He healed the paralytic. It is told in Matthew 9, Mark 2, and Luke 5. The paralyzed man's friends were trying to get to Jesus, but there were too many people gathered in front of His home. So they climbed onto the roof of the house and tore the roof open so that they could let the man down in front of Jesus.

When Jesus saw the man and his friends, He declared, "Son, your sins are forgiven" (Mark 2:5). His detractors, which were almost always hassling Him, complained and accused Jesus of blasphemy since only God can forgive sins. Jesus then asked them a rhetorical question, "Which is easier, to say to the paralytic, 'Your sins are forgiven,' or to say, 'Rise, take up your bed and walk'?" (v. 9). Of course, they are equally easy to say. Talk is always pretty cheap; anyone can claim to forgive sins. But Jesus backed up His talk with actions. To prove that He had the authority to forgive sins, He healed the guy simply by making a declaration. Just as Jesus can heal a paralytic by His words, so He can also forgive sins by His words.

Can we be certain that Jesus forgives us? Does God actually set aside our guilt just because Jesus says so? Well, if His Word can make the paralyzed walk, then certainly His Word is good. When He says to us "I forgive you," then you can trust that word. That's the whole point of the parable. It teaches us about the forgiveness of sins.

When Jesus was dying on the cross, He said, "Father, forgive them." His request of His Father was specifically made about the people who crucified Him. But the request is broader than that. He was asking His Father in heaven to forgive every sinner who ever lived and whoever would live. When that request was made, "Father forgive them," then, Lloyd, Jesus had you and me in mind. We have sinned just as truly as the people who directly cried out for His blood. Does God forgive us just because Jesus asked? The answer is YES. Jesus is the one who absorbed our sins. Peter says, "He Himself bore our sins in His body" (1 Peter 2:24). That entitles Him to ask forgiveness for us, and it entitles Him to speak forgiveness upon us.

Interestingly, in Matthew's account the story concludes with this noteworthy expression: "When the crowds saw it, they were afraid, and they glorified God, who had given such authority to men" (Matthew 9:8). Notice it says "men" and not simply "a man." Jesus is a man who has authority to forgive sins because He is God. Amazingly, God also gives to men, not just to a single man but to men, the right to forgive sins. Who are these men and how do they forgive sins? I will explain this soon.

At this point in the correspondence, about four months after the letters had begun, Lloyd started attending church with his daughter Liz. I was pleased that perhaps the letters had contributed to this decision and especially pleased that Liz had taken the initiative to bring him to the same congregation he had attended fifty years earlier. So I decided, again, to interrupt the flow of what I was saying to explain to him what he should expect in church. I was also determined to write to him about the Divine Service—Word and Sacrament—since he was receiving again these blessings of God.

◇◇◇◇

The "Miracle" of the Ministry

Letter 27

Jan tells me, Lloyd, that you and Liz have started to attend a church—a Lutheran one no less. I am very pleased for you and pray that you will hear the Word regularly at your church. The Sunday church service is a wonderful thing and a great gift of God. But sometimes people are not completely certain what to expect from it. Let me tell you what the service gives. It is something far greater than any miracle.

As a pastor I have talked to many people who want a miracle in their lives. But there is something more important than miracles. A few weeks back people were praying for a miracle in your life, Lloyd, since you were at death's door. But the three miracles that I have told you about show us that miracles in the Bible always point to something far more important than the immediate and awe-inspiring effects of the miracle itself. The miracles of the New Testament are not primarily about physical healing, rather, they point to rest for our souls, or the cleansing of our impurities, or the forgiveness of our guilt. All these are given to us by Jesus, who lived and died for us. The good news for us today is that we do not need miracles in order to have these blessings. They come to us in a much more common way.

When I talked to you last June, Lloyd, I asked you what had happened to your faith. I know that you believed at one time. If I recall your answer correctly you said that you had prayed for faith but that God had not provided it. He had not convinced you. And subsequently, we had our discussion on the virgin birth and other miracles.

I told you that prayer is not how faith is engendered or strengthened. Rather, the Bible says, "Faith comes from hearing, and hearing through the Word of Christ" (Romans 10:17). So it is not miracles or dramatic experiences that give us faith. God gives us faith by His Word. We do not struggle our way to faith through prayer or heartfelt seeking. We come to faith through the Word of Christ. Jesus said, "If you abide in My Word, you are truly My disciples" (John 8:31).

God brings His Word to us in a number of ways. When the pastor preaches, he speaks the message of Jesus—the Word of God. Remember the dove I described hanging over the pulpit?

When people are baptized, it is called a "washing of water with the Word" (Ephesians 5:26). You have probably noticed the baptismal font featured prominently in many churches. We give respect to that which is a vehicle for God's Word.

When people receive the Lord's Supper, they are eating and drinking bread and wine to which the words of Christ are added. These words make the meal a "holy communion" in which we eat and drink, along with bread and wine, also the true body and blood of Jesus for the forgiveness of sins. "Drink of it, all of you, for this is My blood of the covenant, which is poured out for many for the forgiveness of sins," says Jesus (Matthew 26:27–28). Remember the little windows in the chancels of those ancient churches were there so that even people dying of leprosy could enjoy this "meal of immortality" as it has often been called.

These gifts of the Word, Baptism, and the Lord's Supper may seem mundane compared to the miracle of raising someone from the dead. But they are far better. Jan told me that you were baptized in a river as a young boy. This Baptism was a washing of life that purified you. It was God's Word connected with water, and it forgave you for your whole life long. You have sat, I'm sure, through many sermons. I am also sure that you were not always impressed by them or even moved by them. But if the preaching taught you of Jesus and the forgiveness of sins, then God was giving you something greater than any miracle. You have taken the Lord's Supper many times I am sure. And I am also fairly confident that the routine of going to Holy Communion has bred in you a certain disinterest that often accompanies those things that are habitual among us. But the Lord's Supper is still the body and blood of Jesus for the forgiveness of sins. It is still the Word of God for us. It still effects more profoundly, at least in the eyes of heaven, than any of Christ's signs and wonders.

These blessings—Baptism, God's Word of forgiveness, and Holy Communion—are the ways in which God serves us and works in us today. They are the ministry of Christ to us. They forgive sins and build up our faith. And they are much more available than any miracle.

The Greatest Miracle That Never Happened (Part One)

Letter 28

Again, Lloyd, I am very pleased to hear that you are attending church. And as I said last time, the primary purpose of the Divine Service is for God to speak the forgiveness of sins to His people through the Word and Sacraments of Baptism and the Lord's Supper. Please allow me some thoughts about the Word that is to be preached in church.

The Word of God that you hear from the pulpit should always explain to you the single most important event recorded in the Bible: the crucifixion. The crucifixion is the greatest miracle that never happened. (Don't misunderstand me—the crucifixion actually took place; it just wasn't miraculous, as I'll explain.)

The three miracles that I explained a few letters ago all had lessons far more significant than the miracles themselves. (1) That we have our rest in Christ and that we don't have to work our way into His good graces. (2) That we are cleansed in Christ and that He has absorbed all of our impurities. (3) That Jesus forgives us by His Word. All three of these miracles, along with the other miracles Jesus performed, point to an event that was singularly non-miraculous: the crucifixion of Christ. The cross is what the Christian religion is really all about.

While Jesus was dying on the cross, the bystanders, the soldiers, and even the other criminals mocked Him. "If You are the Son of God, come down from the cross. . . . He saved others; He cannot save Himself. He is the King of Israel; let Him come down now from the cross" (Matthew 27:40, 42). What an interesting scenario. Here you have the man who has claimed to be the greatest miracle worker of all times dying on the cross, apparently unable to help Himself. Wouldn't a miracle worker jump at the chance to save himself, proving his powers? However, this was not the first time Jesus refused to perform a miracle.

Earlier in His life, Jesus was very hungry, and the devil tempted Him to turn a stone into bread. "If You are the Son of God, command this stone to become bread" (Luke 4:3). But Jesus refused. Why would He refuse to help Himself?

The answer is back at the cross. Jesus did not come into the world to do miracles. The real mission of Jesus was to die.

Picture Jesus on the last day of His life. Christians call it Good Friday, but it was anything but good for Jesus. He has been forced to stay up all night since being arrested late on Thursday evening. He is paraded from one unjust court to another in the middle of the night. First the Jewish court condemns Him. Then Pilate, the Roman governor of Judea, tries to pawn Him off on Herod, the governor of Galilee, which was Jesus' home. Herod just wants to see a miracle. But Jesus again refuses, even though it might have freed Him. Pilate is pressured by the mob to condemn Him, so he has Jesus whipped, hoping to placate the bloodthirsty mob. The flogging consists of thirty-nine lashes from a whip with stones or sharp pieces of metal attached to nine strips of leather. So Jesus has to endure both terrible pain and complete humiliation. The result of this whipping is that Jesus has been reduced to a bloody mess. All this is experienced by the greatest miracle worker of all times. Why would He allow this?

The flogging does not placate the crowd, and Jesus is condemned to execution outside the city. Battered, bleeding, and weak, He was even forced to carry the cross He would be hung on out of the city and up a hill to the place of His own execution. And this is where the real pain commences.

The Greatest Miracle That Never Happened (Part Two)

Letter 29

When Jesus reaches the top of the hill, the soldiers take the crossbeam that, due to Christ's weakened condition, was forced upon another man to carry. They pound nails through His hands. These nails might have been placed just above the wrists and the soldiers might have also tied Him to the crossbeam. That way His hands would not rip away from the nails when they were forced to bear the full weight of His body. The soldiers hoist Jesus up to the cross and secure the beam. They nail His feet in place to prolong the crucifixion. There He hangs.

Jesus has had no water for about eighteen hours. He has not slept for about thirty hours. He is naked and exposed to both enemies and erstwhile friends. His head, upon which they had placed the infamous crown of thorns, has bled profusely, resulting in a face covered with His own blood. His hair and beard are caked with His own dried blood. His back bears the scars of the whipping recently administered with sadistic efficiency. He's been hit on the head and slapped on the face (the deepest insult you could render in the Mediterranean world).

Doesn't it seem that this might have been a good time for a miracle?

Seven hundred years before the time of Christ, a prophet named Isaiah described the death of a man whom God would send for His people. This man was called the "Suffering Servant." With uncanny precision Isaiah describes His death:

> He was despised and rejected by men; a man of sorrows, and acquainted with grief; and as one from whom men

> hide their faces He was despised, and we esteemed Him not. Surely He has borne our griefs and carried our sorrows; yet we esteemed Him stricken, smitten by God, and afflicted. But He was pierced for our transgressions; He was crushed for our iniquities; upon Him was the chastisement that brought us peace, and with His wounds we are healed. (Isaiah 53:3–5)

This description of Christ's death, penned seven hundred years before it occurred, was a miracle. No one could predict the event with such accuracy. But the death of Christ was itself not miraculous—still it accomplished much more than a miracle. Lloyd, the message of Christ is not that a miracle can be worked in your life. Nor is it that a bunch of miracles were done two thousand years ago by an enigmatic man in a strange land. The message of Christ is that His innocent and painful death was actually used by God for your benefit. Let me paraphrase that last verse of the passage above so that its meaning is plain: He was pierced because of your offenses against God. He was crushed to take away your guilt. He was punished so that you could have peace with God. His wounds have healed you of your sin.

This forgiveness is not accomplished by a miracle. It is accomplished because Jesus refused to do a miracle. He knew that He could either save Himself by a miracle or He could save you by His bitter pain and death. He chose you over Himself.

Faith in Jesus is not the acceptance of miracles—though no Christian would deny them. Faith in Jesus is trusting in His terrible death. That's what makes you a Christian.

◇◇◇◇

He Dies Willingly

Letter 30

The death of Christ occurred rather quickly and almost suddenly compared to other crucifixions. That requires a bit of analysis.

John tells us that the Jewish leaders did not want to desecrate their Sabbath by leaving naked and dying men on the cross. Recall that the crucifixion took place on Friday. By Jewish custom the Sabbath day actually began on Friday evening at 6:00 p.m. and ended the same time on Saturday evening. So it was important to them that their wicked business would come to an end before 6:00 p.m. that day. They convinced Pilate to have the legs of the three men broken. The soldiers complied and broke the legs of the two criminals who were crucified with Jesus. Surprisingly, they found Jesus already dead. His execution began at 9:00 a.m. and six hours later He was dead. How did death happen so soon?

Perhaps it was Jesus' weakened condition. He had been whipped. He had been deprived of food and water. He was sleep deprived. But there is a more profound answer. Jesus died quickly simply because He willed Himself to die.

Earlier in His ministry Jesus had said, "No one takes [My life] from Me, but I lay it down of My own accord. I have authority to lay it down, and I have authority to take it up again" (John 10:18). That means that others did not foist His death upon Him. He was not an unwillingly participant in this drama. Unlike the other criminals, Jesus chose to be on the cross. And, unlike the criminals, He was actually in control of the entire affair. Jesus was dying on the cross not simply because He was the victim of hatred, injustice, and cowardice. He was suffering by His choice. And when the suffering was finished, He died by His choice.

The last word Jesus spoke on the cross in the Gospel of John is the word "It is finished" (John 19:30). (In Greek the phrase "It is finished" is actually only one word.) When it was finished there was no reason for

Him to continue. Once He had suffered enough, He simply chose to die. That is why the soldiers did not need to kill Him quickly by breaking His legs. He had already finished it.

What is the "it" that He had finished?

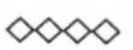

WHAT IS "IT"?

Letter 31

When Jesus said, "It is finished," He was partly referring to His pain and suffering. He had suffered enough. The suffering was now over. But there is much more to the phrase than that.

I can think of at least three things that are included in the word "it." During these next three letters I want you to keep in mind that Jesus claimed to be the Son of God and proved it by His resurrection. That means that these next three letters are based on the claims of God Himself. They are not burdensome lessons; they offer you great encouragement and assurance.

First, "it" is Jesus carrying the sin of the world. He had come into the world to carry our sins and now He was finished with that job. "Behold, the Lamb of God, who takes away the sin of the world!" (John 1:29). John the Baptist spoke that phrase at the very beginning of Christ's ministry. He was saying, "Look at the Lamb of God who is (right now) carrying the sin of the world." That means that Jesus had taken upon Himself all of our offenses against God. It's the same idea as was taught in the miracles of touching, which I mentioned above. It is as if Jesus absorbed the uncleanness of all people. The section of Isaiah I quoted a few letters ago declares, "He bore the sin of many" (Isaiah 53:12). Actually, Lloyd, you should take the time to read that entire section of the Bible from Isaiah 52:13—53:12. It talks about the servant of God (Christ) who will bear the sins of the world.

Probably the best expression for Christ bearing our sins is in 1 Peter 2:24: "He Himself bore our sins in His body on the tree." So when the body of Jesus was punished, your sins were also being punished. And when the body of Jesus was laid into the cold stone tomb on that Good Friday, then that is precisely where your offenses against God were placed. But when

Jesus was raised on Easter Sunday morning, your trespasses against God were left in the grave.

Psalm 103 beautifully talks about forgiveness. There David says, "As far as the east is from the west, so far does He remove our transgression from us" (v. 12). You may have heard Christians say, "Look to the east." We look to the east because that is the place, according to the psalm, where God has removed our sins. We also look east because that is where the Son rises. Note the play on words: the sun rises and the Son rises. Every Christian looks to the resurrection, when the Son of God rose from the dead. There is an old Christian burial custom of making headstones on graves face east, thinking that when Jesus comes again and raises the dead, they will be able to sit up and look directly east without craning their necks. Christians look "east" with the positive assurance that our sins have been carried by Jesus and placed far, far away—so far that they will never accuse us or condemn us again.

What Else Is "It"?

Letter 32

But there is more to Jesus' expression, "It is finished."

"It" is the accusation of God's Law. If Jesus has taken away our offenses, then there is nothing for which we can be accused. When Jesus says, "It is finished," He is saying that all legitimate accusations against us have ended.

Theologians use an old Latin saying: "*Lex semper accusat,*" which means, "The law always accuses." There is a lot of truth to this old saying. Whenever we hear the Law, we feel guilty. When I was a kid watching TV at night, my mom would ask, "Have you finished your homework?" The question accused me because I knew that I had not really finished. I knew the rules: no TV until your homework is done! That rule declared me guilty. The other week a cop stopped me for speeding. Even before my car had rolled to stop on the side of the road I was feeling accused. I knew the law: 55 miles per hour. I knew my offense: 72 in a 55. I was accused by the law and found guilty.

That's the way of God's Law too. It always accuses me. Jesus said, "You have heard that it was said to those of old, 'You shall not murder' . . . But I say to you that everyone who is angry with his brother will be liable to judgment" (Matthew 5:21–22). I know, Lloyd, that both you and I are fairly even-tempered guys. But Jesus accuses us if we hold a grudge or if we simply "let the sun set on our anger."

Jesus also said, "You have heard that it was said, 'You shall love your neighbor and hate your enemy.' But I say to you, Love your enemies and pray for those who persecute you" (Matthew 5:43–44). Well, I feel accused by these words. My prayer life is not particularly stellar even when it comes to friends and family. And I typically complain about my enemies more than I pray for them. When Luther gave an explanation of the First Commandment, he said, "We should fear, love, and trust in God above all things." Again, I feel accused. I think that any honest person would also feel accused. We simply do not love God more than ourselves. We place ourselves first. Our advertisements say, "Because I'm worth it." They do not say, "Because God is worth it." We look out for number one—ourselves.

Now listen to the apostle Paul as he tells us that these accusations of the Law are a thing of the past because of Jesus' death: "When the fullness of time had come, God sent forth His Son, born of a woman, born under the law, to redeem those who were under the law. . . . Christ redeemed us from the curse of the law by becoming a curse for us—for it is written, 'Cursed is everyone who is hanged on a tree' " (Galatians 4:4–5; 3:13). Paul is telling us that Jesus took the accusation for us. He was accused of what we had done against the Law so that we could escape accusation.

Jesus said, "It is finished." That means that accusations against us are now gone because of Jesus. He has taken the accusations and died because of them. Paul says, "There is therefore now no condemnation for those who are in Christ Jesus" (Romans 8:1).

What More Is "It"?

The Passover

Letter 33

"It" is our sin. Jesus has finished carrying away our sin. "It" is also any accusations against us. Jesus has finished removing any condemnation. There is yet another "It": our redemption. To redeem means to pay a price necessary to free someone from slavery. The best way to explain redemption is through the story of the Passover.

When the people of God were brought out of Egypt into the Promised Land, their cross-country trek began with an event called the Passover. The people were treated as slaves in Egypt and oppressed severely by one of the Egyptian Pharaohs. God afflicted the king of Egypt and his people with any number of plagues to pressure Pharaoh into letting the Hebrews, God's people, go into freedom (Exodus 7–11). He sent flies, frogs, and boils, but Pharaoh would not relent. God turned the sun dark and the river to blood. Each time the king would relent, only to change his mind when the plague was past. The plagues were God's way of insulting the false gods of the Egyptians, who worshiped the river and the sun and various other fertility gods and goddesses whom the true God dominated through the miracles of the plagues.

Finally, God procured the freedom of His people through a singular destructive act. He prescribed the Passover (Exodus 12).

God instructed the people to choose a spotless, male, one-year-old lamb from among their flocks. They were to bring it into their homes and treat it almost like a family member. The little kids would even play with the lambs. Then, on the prescribed day, they were to slaughter the lamb and prepare a meal with it. If a family could not afford a lamb, then two or three families could work together on the meal.

The meat from the lamb was to be eaten along with unleavened bread and certain bitter herbs and spices. The bread had to be unleavened—without yeast—as a sign that they were ready to leave at any time. You could not just sit around and wait for the yeast to rise. You were to eat with your outer cloak tucked into your waist so that at any time you could move quickly. The people of God were to be ready at all times for their journey.

The lamb's blood was to be painted on the doorposts of the house. At midnight of that fateful evening God sent an angel of death. Any household that did not have blood on the door suffered the death of the firstborn. However, God "passed over" every house with blood on its door.

Pharaoh and his son were thought to be gods. But the son of the false god lay dead at the hands of the true God. With such defeat and death surrounding him, Pharaoh finally relented and released the Jews. Having been prepared for such an event for days, the Jews left slavery on their way to freedom.

God redeemed His people from slavery through the blood of the Passover lamb, who paid the price necessary to procure their freedom.

What More Is "It"?

Our Redemption

Letter 34

In the Old Testament, the blood of a lamb saved the people from death. In the New Testament the blood of Jesus, the Lamb of God, saves us all from eternal death. Let me tell you about what happened after the Passover.

God told the people that they should remember and observe the manner in which He had redeemed them by following a certain divinely ordained custom. They were to "set apart to the LORD all that first opens the womb. All the firstborn of your animals that are males shall be the LORD's. . . . Every firstborn of man among your sons you shall redeem" (Exodus 13:12–13). This meant that if you had a sheep and it gave birth to a male lamb you were to slaughter the lamb and eat it as a reminder of that lamb which gave his life to redeem the people those many years ago. If you had a donkey and the donkey gave birth, that male donkey colt belonged to God. You redeemed it by sacrificing a lamb. If a young couple gave birth to a firstborn son, then that son belonged to God. You redeemed the son by sacrificing a lamb. So the idea of paying a price to free your children through the death of a spotless lamb was an idea built into the way the people thought and lived. Therefore, when Jesus was born, His earthly parents, Mary and Joseph, went to the temple in Jerusalem and made the obligatory sacrifice for their firstborn Son. It was a vital sacrifice for God's people.

Now let's go back to Calvary and the cross of Christ. In fact, let's go back to a week before the crucifixion. Jesus has been designated "The Lamb of God" (John 1:29) at the beginning of His ministry. He has lived among the children of God and they have initially accepted and loved Him just as the children of the Jewish families back in Egypt would play with the lambs destined for sacrifice. He is spotless—without any sin. It is spring, when the annual celebration of the Passover was about to occur. At the time of Christ, the custom was that about a week prior to the celebration of the Passover in Jerusalem the shepherds would herd thousands of lambs into the city for the annual slaughter and celebration of the Passover. One year—the year Christ died—a smaller procession takes place alongside the running of the lambs. We call it Palm Sunday. On this day Jesus comes into town, surrounded by thousands of spotless yearling lambs. And the people sing a song to Him as He travels to His own slaughter: "Hosanna to the son of David. Blessed is He who comes in the name of the Lord. Hosanna in the highest." "Hosanna" is a Hebrew word that means, "He saves."

Picture the scene. A spotless human sacrificial lamb approaches His death amidst thousands of spotless lambs. The people hail Him as Savior, but will later cry for His blood.

Jesus is the spotless lamb whose blood protects us from the anger of God justly provoked. His blood is not placed on the doorposts of our houses, but it is poured out to redeem us. We are the firstborn sons of God, redeemed by Jesus to belong to God as His children. When Jesus said, "It is finished," He was saying that He had paid with His life the price necessary for us to be the sons of God. "It is finished," means that you belong to God because of Jesus.

Luther wrote something that many Lutheran confirmation students memorize:

> I believe that Jesus Christ, true God, begotten of the Father from eternity, and also true man, born of the Virgin Mary, is my Lord, *who has redeemed* me, a lost and condemned person, purchased and won me from all sins, from death, and from the power of the devil; not with gold or silver, but *with His holy, precious blood and with His innocent suffering and death, that I may be His own* and live under Him in His kingdom and serve Him in everlasting righteousness, innocence, and blessedness. (*Small Catechism*, Second Article)

"It is finished," means you belong to God.

◇◇◇◇

Letter 35

We don't have an annual slaughter and sacrifice of lambs today, but we do still have a Passover. It is slightly different and much better. Let me explain.

In the Old Testament, God commanded His people to remember the night the angel of death passed over their houses. The people were to have a special meal of lamb, bitter herbs, unleavened bread, and wine, while recounting the story of the Passover. They also sang songs, typically taken from Psalms 111 to 118. The most common psalm for the celebration of the Passover was Psalm 118. The whole family traditionally sang this during the Passover meal. Toward the end of the psalm the people would sing, "Save us, we pray, O LORD! O LORD, we pray, give us success! Blessed is He who comes in the name of the LORD!" (vv. 25–26).

Where have we heard these words before? Well, we heard them from the lips of the people who praised Jesus as He came into Jerusalem intent to die for them (Luke 19:38). And they are hopefully familiar to you from another source. One of the songs in the Lutheran liturgy is called the Sanctus, and it is sung just before the people take Communion:

> Holy, holy, holy Lord God of pow'r and might: Heaven and earth are full of Your glory. Hosanna. Hosanna. Hosanna in the highest. Blessed is He who comes in the name of the Lord. Hosanna in the highest. (*LSB* 161)

The first part is from Isaiah 6; the second part is from Psalm 118. It was sung at the annual celebration of the Passover, and it was sung just prior to the death of Christ, our Passover Lamb. Today, it is sung whenever Christians go to Holy Communion. It has been sung for thousands of years. It is a song that says that God is our Savior in Christ because He has redeemed us by the shedding of blood.

In the Old Testament, the blood was placed on the doorposts of the people's houses. But God has something more intimate in mind for the people who celebrate the new Passover in Christ. He places the true blood of the Lamb on our lips and tongues: "Take, drink, this is the blood of the New Testament, which is shed for many for the forgiveness of sins." You celebrate and acknowledge this wonderful gift by singing the song that was sung when the lambs were sacrificed in the Old Testament and the song that was sung just before Jesus was sacrificed for us on the cross.

Lloyd, I want to tell you the two great high points of the worship service. The first is the news from the pulpit that "It is finished." I trust you hear a sermon about the forgiveness of sins every Sunday. The second high point is the Lord's Supper. There you get the true body and blood of Jesus for the forgiveness of sins. No matter what else you get in church, those are the two most important things, and they are from God.

Letter 36

Lloyd, I'd also like to tell you about the Invocation, which occurs at the beginning of the Divine Service. We tend to not appreciate the Invocation fully.

Most services open with a hymn, but the real start of the service is when the pastor says, "In the name of the Father and of the Son and of the Holy Spirit." That oft-quoted little phrase occurs only one time in the Bible. Jesus said, "Go therefore and make disciples of all nations, baptizing them in the name of the Father and of the Son and of the Holy Spirit" (Matthew 28:19). When you were baptized, these words were spoken. What does Baptism do for us?

The word *baptize* means "to wash." When you were baptized, God was taking the forgiveness of sins that Jesus earned for you through His death and intimately applying this forgiveness to you. Just as He washed away our sins on the cross, so He washes them away in Baptism. Jesus earned and accomplished forgiveness on the cross. He applies and gives forgiveness in Baptism. (This is similar to the Lord's Supper. He earned forgiveness when He shed His blood on the cross and He gives forgiveness when we drink the blood in Holy Communion.) That is why the Bible says, "Rise and be baptized and wash away your sins, calling on His name" (Acts 22:16). Notice that Baptism washes away our sins through "the name of the Father and of the Son and of the Holy Spirit." Every time you hear the words of the pastor opening the service you are being reminded of the forgiveness of sins that is yours through your Baptism into Christ.

Sometimes we use the word *christen* when we baptize people, which has the name Christ in it. The word *Christ* is a Greek word that means "anointed one." When you were "christened" you were given the name

"Christian" at your Baptism because that is when God adopted you as His son and became your loving Father.

Baptism is when God placed His name upon you. Just as you became the son of your parents at your birth, so you became a "son of God" at your Baptism. (We are adopted sons; Jesus is the natural son.) That is why the Bible often will refer to Baptism as the "new birth" or the "second birth" (John 3:3–5, Titus 3:4–6). People sometimes disparage the Baptism of children or infants. They say that Baptism cannot be important if you do not remember it or if it was not something you chose. But you don't remember your birth, and that was important. And you did not choose your parents, but they are certainly important. So even if you don't remember your Baptism, it is still crucial. And it is still a wonderful work of God, even though you may not have chosen it. I have personally discovered that most of the great blessings in life were not the things I chose. Every time you hear the words of the Invocation at the beginning of the service you are reminded that God has placed His name upon you. In fact He is placing His name upon you again and again through that brief blessing.

Baptism forgives our sins in the name of Jesus, and Baptism makes us Christians by placing the name of Jesus upon us. It is like a birth certificate guaranteeing that God is our Father and Jesus is our Brother.

◇◇◇◇

The Benediction

Letter 37

The final words spoken by the pastor, the Benediction, are surely familiar to you: "The LORD bless you and keep you; the LORD make His face shine upon you and be gracious to you; the LORD lift up His countenance upon you and give you peace" (Numbers 6:24–26).

These were the words that God gave to Aaron, the priest, who was to speak them over the people of Israel. All subsequent priests were to bless the people with these words. When God told Aaron to speak these words, He also promised, "So shall they put My name upon the people of Israel, and I will bless them" (Numbers 6:27). So, in the Old Testament God placed His name upon the people through the words of the Benediction. And it is the same today.

Note that the name of God is used three times. God is three in one—Father, Son, and Holy Spirit. The one true God who is three in one gives all the blessings of this life and of the life to come. The thrice-holy God is the Father, Son, and Holy Spirit.

Second, God actually uses His Word to bless us. When the pastor says, "The Lord bless you and keep you," the words place the blessing upon you. When the pastor says, "The Lord be gracious to you," through those words the Lord is being gracious to you. He is forgiving your sins and He is putting His name upon you. When the pastor says, "The Lord lift up His countenance upon you and give you peace," God is placing His favor upon you and is at peace with you through those words.

Everything God does is through His word. "Faith comes from hearing, and hearing through the Word of Christ" (Romans 10:17). In the Lutheran Church we sing a great hymn: "Thy strong Word bespeaks us righteous; Bright with Thine own holiness" (*LSB* 578:3).

We are pleasing to God and enjoy His favor; we are forgiven and at peace; we have His name upon us and rejoice in His grace because He has spoken to us. Consequently, our confidence in Him is based 100 percent on His Word and nothing else.

Even the word *benediction* teaches us this important truth. "Bene" means good, as in benefit. "Diction" is to speak. So a benediction is to speak a good word. God speaks His blessings upon us. God speaks good words upon us and so gives us everything we need for heaven.

In our Sunday morning services we start with the Invocation ("In the name of the Father and of the Son and of the Holy Spirit"), which is a reminder of the name that was placed upon us in Baptism. We end with the Benediction, which is the way God places His name upon us. Throughout the entire service God is speaking love, forgiveness, and acceptance upon us. His acceptance is through what we have also called the "Means of Grace."

Letter 38

Luther often used the expression, "Means of Grace." The word *means* is like the word *wagon*. So the Means of Grace are wagons into which God has placed all the blessings of Jesus. Jesus earned and accomplished your forgiveness on the cross. He brings this forgiveness to you through Baptism, through the Lord's Supper, and through the message of Jesus.

A couple of years ago, Jan and I visited an orchard in Eastern Washington. It was early September, and the apples were ripe and ready. The owner showed us around, gave us some delicious apples, and let us wander among the trees. On the side of the road were huge crates, each of them about half the size of a boxcar. As we talked, a truck came along with a hoisting device and basically grabbed the huge crate, lifting it from the ground and placing it on the trailer of the truck. Our gracious host watched whimsically and commented, "There goes a year's work." When we asked what he meant, he replied, "I work all year growing apples, fertilizing, fighting birds and worms as well as weeds. I test the sugar content of the apples and make sure they are the best apples money can buy. When they are just perfect, I pick them and place them in these crates that you see standing on the side of the road. But all of this is worth nothing unless I can get them to the market. You just saw the truck pick up my apples. That truck and others will take the cargo to the fruit plant where the apples will be sold. They will be eaten fresh or made into juice, cider, or sauce. Some will be dried and others used for seed. But without the trucks everything we do is for nothing."

That's exactly the way it is with God's forgiveness. We call it grace. God has given us grace through the life and death of Jesus. He places His grace and forgiveness into certain "trucks" or "wagons." We call them the Means of Grace. These means correspond to the three prominent pieces of furniture that you will see in your church. These "wagons of forgiveness" are (1) the Word that is preached from every true Christian pulpit; (2) Baptism, which takes place at countless Christian fonts; and (3) the Lord's Supper, which is served and celebrated on Christian altars throughout the world. If you want forgiveness, and, Lloyd, I know you must, then these are where God gives it. If you want your faith strengthened and fed, and I have to believe you do, then this is where you must go.

Luther said,

> We treat of the forgiveness of sins in two ways. First, how it is achieved and won. Second, how it is distributed and given to us. Christ has achieved it on the cross, it is true. But he has not distributed or given it on the cross. He has not won it in the supper or sacrament. There he has distributed and given it through the Word, as also in the gospel, where it is preached. . . . If now I seek the forgiveness of sins, I do not run to the cross, for I will not find it given there. . . . But I will find in the sacrament or gospel the word which distributes, presents, offers, and gives to me that forgiveness which was won on the cross. (AE 40:213–14)

So the historical life of Jesus and His death on the cross for us are like the apples placed lovingly into crates on the side of the road. Baptism, the Word, and the Lord's Supper—these are the trucks that transport God's gifts to you.

In the late fall of 2006 Lloyd was visited by a member of a local evangelical church who, though well-meaning, was saying things that would potentially undermine everything that I was trying to do. Apparently she had exhorted him to make a decision of faith, to invite Jesus into his heart, to set aside his reluctance to believe, etc. And she was telling him that faith could be identified by the feelings that attend it.

This was a terrible turn of events. First, it is patently false and void of comfort, and I did not want my father-in-law to hear it. Second, I had explained the meaning of the cross through a series of letters about the phrase "It is finished" and had moved into a discussion of the Divine Service. This visitor was going to confuse him, distract him, or destroy his faith. Third, Lloyd had already spent altogether too much emotional time and energy trying to analyze his own faith. Now this "evangelist" from some false church was about to turn him back to his own musings. Fourth, Lloyd was not very emotional. How was he going to measure up to the types of conversion experiences that I had read about all too often in the annals of American Evangelicalism? The whole thing was unfair, dangerous, and wrong.

So I decided to write about faith, and then I added a series of letters in which I identified "idols" of American Christianity. Here I contradicted the false understanding of faith that we find in so much of American Evangelicalism. Some of these letters are rather polemical in nature, overtly attacking the false doctrine that Lloyd had heard. When you're talking to family members about Jesus, you sometimes have to contradict those who oppose the Gospel.

True Faith: Having

Letter 39

Lloyd, I'd like to tell you about faith. Faith is nothing more than simply receiving all the treasures of Jesus. Faith is having.

Faith is not doing, feeling, striving, deciding, or otherwise exercising. Faith is having. Paul says, "Now to the one who works, his wages are not counted as a gift but as his due. And to the one who does not work but believes in Him who justifies the ungodly, his faith is counted as righteousness" (Romans 4:4–5). What does this passage mean?

Paul's expression "justifies the ungodly" is the same as "forgives sins." God "justifies us" or gives us the forgiveness of sins not because it is "our due." It is not like my paycheck, which I deserve because I have worked for it. Rather, God gives forgiveness to you and me without us doing anything at all. Faith is the opposite of works. "To the one who does not work but believes in Him." Faith is the absence of working.

There are many churches that define faith as doing something. They say that we must strive. We must decide. We must answer. We must choose. We must experience. We must feel, feel, feel, feel, feel. We must *do*. But Paul says, "We must *have*." In effect he is saying, "God has already done all that is necessary. God has *strived* by going to the cross. God has *decided* to love us from eternity. God has *answered* our helplessness, speaking the Gospel to us. God has *chosen* you in Christ. God has *experienced* suffering and death for you. God has *felt* the blows, the nails, the spear, the abandonment of friends, and the rejection of God. God has *done*. There is no more striving, deciding, answering, choosing, experiencing, or feeling that needs to be done. "It is finished." It's all been done. You must *have*. Here it is. I give it to you, says God. You must have.

Faith is having.

I once compared faith to the bag of a kid collecting candy on Halloween. Just as the bag holds the precious confections of that holiday, so faith holds the precious gifts that God showers on us in Christ. Faith is having the forgiveness of sin through Jesus. Faith is receiving the status of righteous through the Word of God. Faith is possessing the promise of heaven and holding that promise. Faith is having.

In America we are encouraged to agonize over faith and wonder whether our faith is strong enough. We are spiritual narcissists. We indulge our egos by thinking that we have to do or feel or experience. But what we really need is to be given, to be loved, to be forgiven, and to have. You, Lloyd, were filled with angst analyzing the reality of your faith the last time I saw you. I would advise that you quit thinking about faith and think more about Jesus, who suffered, died, and rose again for us.

True Faith: Knowledge

Letter 40

To have faith and to believe are the same thing. They come from the same Greek word in the Bible. The English translations of the Bible typically use the word *faith* to translate the Greek noun and the word *believe* to translate the Greek verb. Sometimes instead of saying "believe," they will say "have faith" or they will use the word *trust.* But the three are the same.

Theologians have often said that true faith involves three things: knowledge, assent, and trust. What do these three things mean? *Knowledge* is having the data, the facts, the information about God, and especially the information of the Good News of the forgiveness of sins through Jesus. *Assent* is agreeing and holding on to the Good News of Jesus. *Trust* means that you have confidence in the knowledge. You rely on the Gospel. You believe God has done these things specifically for you.

All three of these are necessary in order to have true faith. So let's start with knowledge. I have told you much about Jesus' miracles, His crucifixion, His resurrection, God's Word, Baptism, and the Lord's Supper. These are the things that God has done for us or given to us. To have faith you must know them.

Knowledge is that characteristic of faith which yearns to attend church and learn more about Christianity. And it is that aspect of faith that gets angry when you go to church and don't learn anything about Jesus or His forgiveness. It is that side of faith which would attend Bible class or read the Bible daily. True faith possesses knowledge of Christ and craves more knowledge about Him.

◇◇◇◇

True Faith: More about Knowledge

Letter 41

I think that, at least historically, the Lutheran Church has done very well in attempting to satisfy the desire for knowledge that resides in every Christian soul.

The hymns we sing teach about Jesus and about some aspect of the Christian faith. Lutheran preachers are trained to impart knowledge in their sermons and to apply the knowledge of the Bible to people's lives. Martin Luther translated the Bible so that the common people could actually read it. Before his time it was available only in Latin, which was the language of academia but not the language of the streets. Luther also took the Roman Latin Mass and translated it into German because he wanted the people to understand what God was giving them through the Divine Service. The fact that you can read the Bible and can understand the liturgy in your own language is something for which you can thank Martin Luther. It was important that the people have knowledge.

Probably the greatest educational tool in the history of the Christian Church was written by Martin Luther as well: the Small Catechism. It is short—about ten pages—and is used to teach the Ten Commandments, the Apostles' Creed, the Lord's Prayer, Baptism, forgiveness (or the Absolution), and the Lord's Supper.

Lutheran congregations in America, at least those of The Lutheran Church—Missouri Synod, have historically supported the largest primary and secondary school system in the country relative to the size of the church body. We do this because we are convinced that an important aspect of faith is knowledge.

I am very blessed to be a pastor because my job is to teach the knowledge of Jesus and this requires of me that I learn. So I get to spend my days acquiring more and more knowledge about Christ and His Word. I get excited when I am studying a section of the Bible and I gain a new insight. I am thrilled with the study of doctrine, especially when some ancient theologian gives me an insight that I had not previously had.

If you have lost your faith, Lloyd, it is simply because the flow of knowledge has been stopped. God has a hundred ways of imparting the knowledge of His grace in Christ. It is always through His Word. The flow must resume if knowledge is to be gained.

True Faith: Knowing God

Letter 42

Sometimes the word *know* means "to have information about." I know what the capital of California is. I know that three plus four equals seven.

However, sometimes the word *know* means "to have a relationship with." I know that George W. Bush is a former president, but if asked, "Do you know George Bush?", I would say, "Well not really. I have never met the guy." On the other hand, if you asked me whether I know my wife Jan Preus, I would say, "Yes, of course I know her. We have an intimate relationship. In some ways I know her better than she knows herself." The word *know*, in this context, is much more than the possession of information and data.

In the Bible, God tells us that He *knows* us. He has intimate awareness of every aspect of our lives. He knows how we think and feel. He knows our needs far better than we do and provides them more pointedly than we even appreciate. The word *know* in this case means the same as "have an intimate awareness and care." In the Bible God can even go so far as to say that He "knew" us before the creation of the world (Romans 8:29).

Do you know God? Many people would answer, "Well, yes. I have certain information about Him. I know the content of the Bible pretty well. I know the stories of the miracles and the history of Jesus. I suppose I know God."

But to truly know God is to have Him and hold Him, to possess and treasure Jesus. Faith is having Jesus and knowing Him as the wonderful treasure He is. "This is eternal life," says Jesus, "that they know You the only true God, and Jesus Christ whom You have sent" (John 17:3).

I was once examining some kids in preparation for receiving Communion for the first time. I asked one of them, "What does Jesus mean to you?" He squirmed in his chair, looked at the ceiling, knit his brow, and finally said in frustration, "I know this one, just give me a bit of time. I know this. It will come to me." I would suggest the kid might actually have been able to pass a test of his knowledge about Jesus. But I worried that he really did not know Jesus.

Faith is having Jesus and having an intimate knowledge of Him.

True Faith: Assent

Letter 43

Faith also means that we agree with the promises of God. Theologians have often called this "assent," which means that we accept something as true. I once heard a professor correctly say, "Faith is not simply that we believe in God; it also means that we believe God." Faith is to say, "I concur." It's saying, "Yes, if God says so, then it must be so."

Now it seems to me that this is actually pretty close to what we discussed last summer. God says certain things about us, about the world, and about Himself in the Bible. Faith is not that we accept these things because they make sense. Faith is not that we accept things because we have experienced them. Faith is not that we accept things because they correspond to the considered opinions of academically credentialed persons. Faith is believing something simply because God says so. That's assent.

Earlier, I explained why it is reasonable to believe that Jesus rose from the dead. If you recall, I claimed it was the only sensible explanation of the data as we have it. But if you believe that Jesus died and rose simply because it is reasonable and because you cannot present a better explanation of the facts, then you really do not have faith. True faith believes in the life, death, and resurrection of Jesus because God says so.

When I was a kid my brother Danny and I would play softball or football with the kids in the neighborhood after school. Sometimes one of the kids on the opposing team would falsely tell us that our dad was calling us to dinner. "I think I heard your dad calling you home." We would not believe him. We had no faith in what others claimed was the call of Dad. We distrusted the motives of those who announced it. They simply wanted us to leave and return two minutes later, which would give them the opportunity to win the game. Actually, Dad had a rather unique way of calling us to dinner. He emitted a high piercing whistle that would echo and resound throughout the neighborhood. He instructed us that we would know when dinner was served by the whistle. So we had faith in the whistle because we had faith in Dad. When we heard that sound, we knew what it meant, and we assented to it. We agreed with it. We concurred that it was dinnertime.

That's the way faith is. Faith agrees with God when He speaks. Faith concurs with the Word of God, which He speaks to us in Christ. Faith hears the precious Gospel of forgiveness through Christ as taught in the Bible, and faith says, "Yes, I know Jesus and I know the Bible and I know that He has forgiven my sins."

Assent is that aspect of faith which will take God at His Word even when it does not make sense or when it makes you feel uncomfortable. There are things that God says in the Bible that are politically incorrect by today's ever-changing standards. True faith would rather be politically incorrect than believe something different from what God says. There are teachings in the Bible that seem almost un-American. I will come to these in a couple of days. True faith shrugs and says, "I agree with what God says even though it flies in the face of American sensibilities."

There was a nineteenth-century philosopher named Immanuel Kant. He asserted that the most outrageous claim in the Bible is that God gives His law and then chooses to forgive us even though we have not complied with His law. That made no sense at all to Immanuel Kant, arguably the most intelligent man of the century. Many intelligent people agreed with him, and many in the Church simply abandoned the faith. They thought it was foolishness to believe that we can actually escape the consequences of our own disobedience. But God says that in Christ we can. Jesus has obeyed God for us. So should I agree with Kant and most of the intelligent people of the world, or should I agree with God, who created and redeemed me?

◇◇◇◇

True Faith: Trust

Letter 44

"Trust" in Jesus is confidence that everything He did during His life and death were intended FOR YOU.

Faith listens to the story of Christ giving rest to the souls of those burdened with guilt. And faith says, "The rest that Christ gives is FOR ME."

Faith hears the story of Jesus who touched the unclean and absorbed their diseases, and faith says, "The cleansing that Christ affects is FOR ME."

Faith heeds the words of Jesus to those paralyzed with sin and immobilized by their own foibles, and faith is confident that the healing of those paralyzed is really "FOR ME."

Anyone who reads the story of the passion and death of Christ will react with a certain and visceral indignation and sympathy. We should all be angry when a good man is treated so unjustly. Everyone winces as they develop a mental picture of the beatings and the various sadistic machinations of the soldiers. We hear of the crown of thorns and instinctively say, "Ouch." We wonder at the wounds in His hands and feet and recoil in empathy. We contemplate the spear thrust summarily, almost casually, into His side and it really makes us a bit uncomfortable. But all of this analysis, however compassionate and understanding, is not faith. Faith hears the story of the death of Jesus and adds those two little words, "FOR ME."

Faith sees the crucifixion of Jesus portrayed through paintings or statues and is able to say that all of this happened, "FOR ME."

Faith sees Michelangelo's statue of Mary holding the dead body of Jesus and faith responds with more than an appreciation of the beauty of the art. Faith is more than sorrow that it had to happen. Faith is more than admiration of Jesus or feelings of grief for His mother. Faith says He is dead "FOR ME."

My favorite hymnwriter is a man named Paul Gerhardt, who lived in the seventeenth century. One of his greatest hymns is entitled, "Upon the Cross Extended." Listen to the lyrics.

> Your soul in griefs unbounded,
> Your head with thorns surrounded,
> It crushed me to the ground.
> The cross for me enduring,
> The crown for me securing,
> My healing in Thy wounds is found.
>
> A crown of thorns Thou wearest,
> My shame and scorn Thou bearest,
> That I might ransomed be.
> My Bondsman, ever willing,
> My place with patience filling,
> From sin and guilt hast made me free. (*LSB* 453:5 and *TLH* 171:6–7—I combined certain stanzas of the hymn in order to maximize the use of the phrase "for me" as I wrote to Lloyd.)

Faith is the capacity to add the words "FOR ME" to all that Jesus did through His life and death.

American Idol: Reason

Letter 45

Now that I have spent a number of letters talking about faith, it seems wise to talk about the idols that tempt us to question or deny Jesus, who is the object of our faith.

I watched *American Idol* last night. I trust you have seen it. In it thousands of contestants demonstrate their singing skill (or lack thereof) in an attempt to become a singing star. They call these stars "Idols" because we tend to treat them almost like gods, worshiping them and showering upon them the devotion that rightly only belongs to God Himself. Well, pop stars are not the only idols to which Americans are drawn.

Idols have competed with Jesus in every place and every era for the past two thousand years. These idols are rarely made of stone or wood. They are usually ideas that seem good but which, upon deep scrutiny, are actually very harmful and very untrue. Let me analyze some of the idols of our day that attempt to deny Jesus.

The first idol that entices people away from Jesus is reason. Everyone has a tendency to question or deny anything that goes against our common sense. So if something doesn't make sense to us, we try to explain it away. Or we try to fit it into categories that do make sense for us. Our reason becomes the thing against which we measure all else. Reason becomes our god.

Obviously, reason can be a good thing. In the catechism that Jan gave you, on the very first page, we thank God for giving "my reason and all my senses" (*Small Catechism*, First Article). It's one thing to thank God for our reason. It's another thing to place reason above God. When we do that, we submit God to our reason rather than the other way around. That's idolatry—the worship of something other than God.

Luther, helpfully, talked about reason in two ways. He talked about the ministerial use of reason and the magisterial use of reason. In the first case reason was used as a servant: your reason and common sense serve you. They are not perfect. Someone else's may be better. God does speak to us in the Bible, and we need our reason to understand the things He says and does. So reason is a minister. It serves.

But when reason becomes a magistrate, it is no longer a servant. Then you serve it and reason has become your lord and your god. Many in the world insist that if they do not understand something, then it cannot be real or true. So God is unreal or untrue if you cannot understand Him.

There are going to be things about God that we simply will not fathom. Just as children do not understand their parents fully, especially when they are young, so we, children of God, will not understand God completely. And just as parents do not see fit always to explain everything they are doing, so God does not see fit to explain Himself fully to us.

We call God "Our Father" in the Lord's Prayer. That is because we trust Him to bless us as any good father would. And we trust Him to provide for us as fathers do. Especially we call God "Our Father" because He gives to us His Son. But another reason we call Him "Father" is because we simply do not always understand His ways. But still we trust, even when we do not understand. That is what it means to call God "Father." It means we place Him above our ability to understand. He is above our reason.

◇◇◇◇

RATIONALISM

Letter 46

In the late eighteenth century and into the nineteenth century there was a philosophical movement in Europe called Rationalism. One of its leading advocates was a philosopher named Immanuel Kant. Kant felt that it was not reasonable to believe that people could be considered guilty for something they personally did not do. Therefore, he denied the ancient doctrine of original sin, which holds that all of us are accountable for the sin of our first parents. Kant also taught that it was completely unreasonable to think that we could find favor with God without actually pleasing Him with our own behavior. Therefore, he denied Jesus Christ, through whom we have the favor of God by the forgiveness of our sins.

Kant placed his own reasoning ability above God. But his rationalism was really nothing more than making an idol of his ability to think. Rationalism was a harsh attack against Christianity.

Rationalism denied miracles and mysteries. Events such as the parting of the Red Sea, or the story of Elijah leaving earth in a chariot of fire were dismissed as folklore. Miracles such as the virgin birth or the resurrection were summarily denied.

The sacraments of Baptism and the Lord's Supper were considered mere human rituals with no divine power or purpose in them. It just didn't make sense to rationalists that you could throw water on a baby, speak the words of Christ, and that little child would become a forgiven child of God. It made no sense that you could take bread and wine, add God's Word, and have it become the body and blood of Jesus in a saving Sacrament of the Altar.

The influence of Rationalism has been immense. Today, millions of people reject the miracles of the Bible because they go against our common sense or experience. Entire church bodies reject Baptism and the Lord's Supper just because they are mysteries. People can't believe that God could work in such a way. It isn't reasonable to them. It doesn't make sense. In this way of thinking, "I become like God." It's just like the Garden of Eden.

You might want to consider, Lloyd, how much this way of thinking has affected you. I know that I struggle against it daily. Everyone who has learned to value his thinking ability and his reason as a "minister" is tempted to view his thinking ability and reason as "Lord." And it is a very heady and formidable temptation.

The attack of Rationalism upon Christianity was nowhere more obvious than in the denial of the nature of God Himself. The rationalists could not accept the biblical teaching of the Trinity: one God—Father, Son, and Holy Spirit. To rationalists, God did not exist simply because they could not understand Him. Common sense had become god. Reason had become their idol.

The Trinity and Reason

Letter 47

When reason is your idol and common sense is your god, you cannot believe anything you do not understand, such as the Trinity. It's a mystery—impossible to understand and impossible to grasp with our paltry human reason. There is one God, who cannot be divided into pieces or parts. He is indivisible. Yet the Bible clearly says that the Father is God, the Son is God, and the Holy Spirit is God. And to make things even more mysterious, the Son is distinct from the Father, the Father is distinct from the Spirit, and the Spirit is distinct from the Son. If that's not confusing enough, you have these mysterious words that describe the relationship between the Three in One: The Son is begotten of the Father from eternity. The Spirit proceeds from the Father and the Son. Yet in all this there are not three gods. There is one God. This is the only God, and there is no other God.

Every Divine Service begins with the words, "In the name of the Father and of the Son and of the Holy Spirit." This formula is from Matthew 28:19. It is the name into which every Christian has been baptized. Notice there is one name. It does not say, "In the names." Rather it says, "Baptizing them in the name of the Father and of the Son and of the Holy Spirit." One name and then three are mentioned—Father, Son, and Holy Spirit. So there are three names in one. And everything in our worship is from the Three in One: the Trinity.

Christians love this triune God. We do not understand the nature of God or the math of the Trinity. But what children fully understand their parents? I suppose some Christians may understand it a bit better than others. And some Christians are able to explain it better. But God is God. You're never going to understand Him fully.

We have a prayer that says:

> It is truly good, right, and salutary that we should at all times and in all places give thinks to You, holy Lord, almighty Father, everlasting God, who with Your only-begotten Son and the Holy Spirit are one God, one Lord. In the confession of the only true God, we worship the Trinity in person and the Unity in substance, of majesty co-equal. Therefore with angels and archangels and with all the company of heaven we laud and magnify Your glorious name. (*LSB Altar Book*, 155)

I am, frankly, not at all sure that this prayer really explains things fully. For me it raises more questions than it answers. But it is not intended to answer all my rationalistic queries. It is intended to place me under the lordship of God—Father, Son, and Holy Spirit. This prayer gives us an opportunity to praise God. After you have thought about the Trinity long enough, you begin to realize that you will never understand Him. But you can confess Him and praise Him.

The triune God is not a God you understand. He is the one and only God whom His children trust and adore. We honor Him whether we understand Him or not. You do not grasp with reason; you grasp with faith. You do not explain; you adore.

So you, and all people, are confronted with a choice, I suppose. Do you want to insist that you will never believe in something you do not understand? Then your understanding is above everything else in the universe. Reason is your god. Or will you accept and love God even though His nature and being are above your comprehension?

Letter 48

If reason has become the god of many, then feelings have become the idol of many more. In fact, the most obvious distinguishing feature of Christianity in America is the worship of feelings.

We could look at feelings much as we look at reason and conclude, like Luther, that feelings can be viewed either as a servant or as a master. Everyone has feelings. God gave them to us, and they are truly a blessing if they serve us and help us. But when feelings become our lord, when they determine or dictate our faith, when we judge God by them, then we have made them an idol.

There is a strong tendency in our country, more so I think than anywhere else in the world, to guide ourselves by feelings. It's the same in our religious sensibilities. The most uniquely American religious invention is a type of worship service in which the people would judge the preacher by how he made them feel. And the preacher would judge his effectiveness by whether or not people would "feel" the presence and power of God. These types of worship services, called revivals, began to develop in the colonial period of our country's history and have evolved since then. One scholar explains that "revivals marked the beginning of the attempt to build a new Christian community united by intense feeling."[6] Feelings have become god. People judge their faith, their doctrine, and God by feelings. This is the way of many television preachers. They believe that faith is predominantly based on feelings and they do everything in their power to get you to feel something. They choose emotional music and preach highly emotive sermons—all so that you can "feel" the grace of Jesus. But Jesus is not something you feel; He is someone you trust. And trust may not always be laden with emotions.

I'm sure that this false god, Lloyd, has probably tempted you. Those who promote this wrong way of believing may have badgered you. Has anyone ever said to you that if you are truly Christian, then you will have a religious experience? That you will experience a feeling of peace in your heart? That you will have a "heart strangely warmed"? Has anyone told you to pray until you feel the presence of God? Have you ever felt a bit out of it or deprived because you don't seem to have the feelings of joy that other Christians do? Have you ever felt like a second-rate Christian because sometimes you think that life is really not all that great? (In fact, sometimes life is actually really, really bad.) Then you are being tempted by the great American idol: feelings.

Those who judge the Christian religion by feelings rather than by the Word of God will almost always disparage or deny the Sacraments. In America there are many churches that will tell you not to trust in Baptism. They believe that since babies do not feel any different upon being baptized, Baptism must not have done much. These false religions will tell adult Christians that they should get re-baptized, as if the first Baptism isn't any good because it didn't create feelings in you. Many Christians have been led to sin against God by being re-baptized. They judge His gracious work in Baptism by their fleeting emotions. They worship feelings instead of Christ.

Many religious groups will also falsely tell you that unless you feel something when receiving Holy Communion, then maybe it was not all that great. But Holy Communion is the true body and blood of Jesus whether we feel it or not.

When you go to the Lord's Supper often, like Christians tend to do, you do not generally feel any different. I have parents at my church who struggle with their kids during the service. When they come to the altar for Communion, they are often distracted and even angry at their errant bundles of joy. They don't feel anything except a bit of numbness (which I think is the absence of feeling). But they are still blessed, and they are still encouraged to trust despite their lack of feeling. If I told these people to judge by their feelings, I would be doing them a huge disservice. Instead, I tell them not to worry about feeling angry or frustrated. Simply trust that Jesus gives you His grace through the body and blood in Communion.

Don't make feelings your idol by placing your trust in them.

◇◇◇◇

Letter 49

Rarely, if ever, are faithful people in the Bible described according to their feelings. Yes, the word *joy* is often used in the Bible to describe those with faith. However, joy, in the Bible, is not a feeling; it is a conviction of well-being in Christ. People rejoice over Jesus and what He has done for them. Think of the heroes in the Bible who had great faith but little feelings.

Samson was a man of superhuman strength. He was tied to the pillars of a pagan temple and forced to listen as his enemies mocked him and his God. Samson prayed for strength just one last time and God gave it to him. He pulled the pillars of the temple in such a way as to collapse the structure and kill God's enemies. How do you think he felt when the falling stone crushed him? The Bible focuses not on Samson's feelings but on his faith and actions. He saved his people and vindicated God by his death (Judges 16:23–31).

How did Jesus feel on the cross? We can imagine that He felt pain, sadness, and emptiness. But again, the Bible focuses not on Jesus' feelings but on His faith and actions. Jesus vindicated God and saved His people from their enemies.

You are not a Christian by feeling. You are a Christian when you are buried with Christ in your Baptism, crucified with Him and raised to a new life (Romans 6:1–11). It is a life in which we suffer with Christ and endure with Christ and trust in Christ. And if we feel like some temple is falling upon us then maybe that is the best thing that could ever happen.

Think of John the Baptist. He preached a hard message of repentance, saying that he must decrease in the presence of the Lord. He seems to have been a rather sober and serious guy, and he was ultimately beheaded for his faithfulness (Matthew 14:1–12). Jesus says that no one born of woman is greater than John the Baptist (Matthew 11:11). Do you think that John the Baptist judged his faith and his Lord by his feelings?

I could mention Moses, who spent half of his ministry complaining to God about the hardheaded people he was supposed to lead. I could mention Jeremiah, who wanted to die when things got so bad. I could mention Jonah, who sat under a tree trying to pout God into doing what he wanted. I could mention Job, who certainly did not spend his days smiling and carrying on about how happy he felt. I could mention Paul, who, when he really wanted to brag about his Christian experiences, listed all the bad things that happened to him. These are the heroes we should emulate, not those who tell you how to feel. Read 2 Corinthians 11:16–12:10. If all Christians would read that passage about Paul's boasting in suffering, and if we would all take it to heart, then no one would ever say again that we should trust our feelings.

Trust Jesus. He is far more consistent and faithful than your feelings. His Word never changes like feelings often do. He loves you and died for you. He promises you grace and forgiveness with no strings attached in His Holy Word and Sacraments.

Letter 50

Probably the biggest danger in trusting your feelings is that such trust often ignores one of the greatest blessings God gives—suffering.

God uses suffering in our lives to make us stronger. Paul says, "We rejoice in our sufferings, knowing that suffering produces endurance, and endurance produces character, and character produces hope, and hope does not put us to shame, because God's love has been poured into our hearts through the Holy Spirit, who has been given to us" (Romans 5:3–5).

God especially commends people and praises them if they suffer for the sake of Christ. Peter says, "Beloved, do not be surprised at the fiery trial when it comes upon you to test you, as though something strange were happening to you. But rejoice insofar as you share Christ's sufferings, that you may also rejoice and be glad when His glory is revealed" (1 Peter 4:12–13). So the greatest Christian skill is not to crave happy feelings or exciting times. The greatest Christian skill is to trust Jesus even when there is great reason to be sad over the pain we feel. God uses that pain to make us strong.

As I look back on my life I can honestly say that the most painful things that I endured—the things I had to suffer—were the best things that ever happened. My father's death, my divorce from my first wife, the various estrangements from friends, and the hassles in congregations and in my church body—these are the things I tried the hardest to avoid. Yet they are the things that made me grow.

I'll bet the same is true of you. As you look at the pain in your life—whether it was the loss of your wife or the times your kids kept you up all night or let you down, whether it was your own recent illness or the illness of someone else. Whether it was the broken promises or broken hearts—these are what God uses to build faith, if we can only see His hand in our lives.

God, in fact, loves us so much He sends adversity and pain our way so that we can learn to put into perspective the things of this life as they compare to heaven. Paul says, "For I consider that the sufferings of this present time are not worth comparing with the glory that is to be revealed to us" (Romans 8:18). Suffering makes us feel crummy and worried or angry or sad or something unpleasant. But it also forces us to look to God's Word. Luther said, "When you no longer accord the Word greater validity than your every feeling, your eyes, your senses, and your heart, you are doomed. . . . I feel and see that I and all other men must rot in the ground; but the Word informs me differently, namely, that I shall rise in great glory and live eternally" (AE 28:70–71).

So trust the Word and trust in the sufferings of Jesus. Trust even that He works in your sufferings. But do not make an idol of your feelings.

American Idol: My Will

Letter 51

The third idol of Americans, and perhaps the most soundly entrenched idol, is our will. In America, because we have accomplished so much, sometimes largely due to the strength of human resolve, we tend to think that salvation is a matter of the human will. But Christianity is not a matter of exercising our will and making a decision for Jesus. Rather the Bible teaches that God, by His endless and boundless love, has made a decision for you. He has loved you in Christ and chosen you. He has committed Himself to you. So strong was His commitment to you that He willingly died on the cross for you. He speaks gently to you, and by that gracious word He turns your heart toward His love.

God does not wait for us to come to Him. He comes to us through His Word and through the promises of Baptism and the Lord's Supper. Just as He created us from nothing simply by the power of His mighty word, so He creates faith in us out of nothing simply by the power of His holy word of grace. That is why the psalmist says, "Create in me a clean heart, O God, and renew a right spirit within me" (Psalm 51:10). And Paul attributes the creation of faith to the word of God with no reference whatsoever to the exercise of our will. "Faith comes from hearing, and hearing through of the word of Christ" (Romans 10:17).

This is important to know and believe because we are inundated with incorrect religious messages that faith is a matter of choice. "Jesus is standing at the door of your heart and is knocking," we are told. "The doorknob is on the inside of your heart. All you have to do is choose to let Him in. Jesus has done His part; now you have to do your part. Simply choose Him to be your Lord and Savior." All of these common beliefs are, quite simply, false.

The apostle John, in talking about how a person comes to faith, says, "To all who did receive Him, who believed in His name, He gave the right to become children of God, who were born, not of blood nor of the will of the flesh nor of the will of man, but of God" (John 1:12–13). I don't think this is such a difficult passage to understand, though it does go against the religious sensibilities of most American thinkers. Faith is a gift of God. It is not something that we inherited through blood or acquired by an act of our will.

Paul says, "By grace you have been saved through faith. And this is not your own doing; it is the gift of God, not a result of works, so that no one may boast" (Ephesians 2:8–9). Faith is a gift. Paul says it again in Romans: "What shall we say then? Is there injustice on God's part? By no means! For He says to Moses, 'I will have mercy on whom I have mercy, and I will have compassion on whom I have compassion.' So then it depends not on human will or exertion, but on God, who has mercy" (Romans 9:14–16). Faith, then, is not a matter of our will, decision, choice, work, or exertion. Faith is worked in us by God and is a gift from Him.

Luther echoes the same in the *Small Catechism*: "I believe that I cannot by my own reason or strength believe in Jesus Christ, my Lord, or come to Him; but the Holy Spirit has called me by the Gospel, enlightened me with His gifts" (*Small Catechism*, Third Article).

Why is this important? Because there is a desire—a latent, desperate, sinful human desire—that resides in every human, to have some credit for the grace that God gives us in Christ. We simply but wrongly want some credit. We want to practice what I call "Little Jack Horner theology." Little Jack, you recall, spent his days sitting in a corner and saying, "Oh, what a good boy am I." Many Christians sit in their various corners and imagine that they are going to heaven because they are such good boys and girls. They decided or made a choice. "God must be pleased with me for my decision," is the thought of some. But the Bible will not allow that type of Christianity.

The Bible says, "Let him who boasts boast in this, that he understands and knows Me, that I am the Lord" (Jeremiah 9:24). God does not want us to brag about any role we imagine we have played in our salvation. He wants us to credit everything to Christ and His Spirit. That is what it means to honor God and to trust in Him. It means to rely on Him for His gift and for the faith that grabs the gift. The gift is Jesus.

◇◇◇◇

Revelation 3:20

Letter 52

The passage invoked more often than any other in an attempt to prove that we must exercise our will in order to be saved is Revelation 3:20. It says, "Behold, I stand at the door and knock. If anyone hears My voice and opens the door, I will come in to him and eat with him, and he with Me." This passage is often purported to teach that Jesus is knocking at the door of our heart and that by an act of the will we must let Him in.

Actually, there is no mention in the passage of the human heart. And the context of the passage shows that Jesus is not knocking at the door of our hearts; He is knocking at the door of the church. This passage is part of a longer section of the Book of Revelation in which John writes to the seven congregations in Asia Minor. In Revelation 3:20 he is writing to the congregation in Laodicea. Earlier in verse 15, John tells the congregation that they are lukewarm. He deplores their lack of commitment and tells them to trust in Christ's riches. He exhorts them to trust solely in Christ. There is nothing worse than a congregation that does not place Jesus front and center in their ministry and in their confidence. The words in Revelation 3:20 are an encouragement to put the message of Jesus and His Sacraments in the center. The words are not an encouragement for an individual to be converted to Christ. They are an encouragement for a Christian congregation to repent and place Jesus first.

The congregation at Laodicea was cocky and self-confident. They thought they were prosperous probably because they had a lot of money. Jesus tells them to find their prosperity in the white garments of His innocence and righteousness that are counted to their credit and that cover the shame of sin. Our wealth is in the forgiveness of sins and the spiritual sight that makes us see Jesus. Revelation 3 is about a church going back to its first love and recommitting itself to Jesus.

Churches are the living flock of Christ, who is the Good Shepherd. And just as flocks can often wander, so congregations—churches—need the constant encouragement to continue to hear the voice of Jesus. What makes people Christians is not choosing or deciding but hearing and listening to the voice of Jesus.

I pray, Lloyd, that the congregation you have found does not have confidence in its own abilities or its own wealth, but that it is a congregation that places the Gospel of Christ in the center and that enjoys the presence of Jesus and "sups with Him" in His blessed Sacrament of the Altar.

Do We Believe in God's Eternal Choice?

Letter 53

In my many years of ministry I have often taught God's people that faith is not our decision but a gift of God. God chooses me through His Word and for the sake of Jesus. Someone inevitably asks, "If it is a matter of God's choice, then why doesn't He simply choose all people to be saved?" Since some people are not Christians, it is claimed, this is proof that it's up to the individual to decide.

Here is how people reason. (Keep in mind that reason is not always the best indicator of what is true.) Either God decides who will go to heaven and who will go to hell, or people decide. If you say that heaven is not my choice but God's, then you must also believe that God has decided who will go to hell. Some religions teach that heaven or hell is a decision of God. Most religions think that heaven or hell is a decision of the individual.

That seems to make sense, but it is not what the Bible teaches. Rather, and paradoxically, the Bible teaches that if a person goes to hell, it is his own obstinate and sinful fault for his sin and his refusal to take hold of the grace God gives him in Christ. But if a person goes to heaven, it is because God has chosen him to go to heaven and has done everything necessary in Christ to get him to heaven.

Jesus weeps over Jerusalem and says, "O Jerusalem, Jerusalem, the city that kills the prophets and stones those who are sent to it! How often would I have gathered your children together as a hen gathers her brood under her wings, and you were not willing!" (Matthew 23:37). It's not that Jesus didn't want His own people in heaven, they simply refused His offer. It's their fault and the fault of everyone who rejects Jesus. "[God] desires all people to be saved and to come to the knowledge of the truth" (1 Timothy 2:4). He would never plan for someone to be in hell.

At the same time, if someone comes to faith, it is the work of God, and only God. Hebrews 12:2 says that we should fix our eyes on Jesus, who is the author and perfecter of our faith. Jesus starts our faith, and He sustains our faith, and He finishes our faith. He does this by feeding it and strengthening it with the same tools He used to create it: His Holy Word and the Sacraments of Baptism and the Lord's Supper.

In Acts 13 there is an intriguing story. Paul and Barnabas preached the word of God to a Jewish community. They were reviled for their efforts. So Paul said, "It was necessary that the word of God be spoken first to you. Since you thrust it aside and judge yourselves unworthy of eternal life, behold, we are turning to the Gentiles. . . . And when the Gentiles heard this, they began rejoicing and glorifying the word of the Lord, and as many as were appointed to eternal life believed" (Acts 13:46, 48). Notice that when people reject, they judge themselves unworthy. They are responsible for their stubborn unbelief. But when people believe, it is because God had "appointed [them] to eternal life." God be praised for salvation. People be judged for sin.

This may seem like a paradox or a mystery impossible to understand. But, as I said, our ability to understand things is not always a guarantee of truth. And our inability to understand does not make something false. If we insist on understanding, we either blame God for what is our fault or we will take credit for something that is God's doing. Both are actions that we should humbly and faithfully avoid.

So do not have confidence in your will or your decision-making ability. They will help you immensely in this life but not for the life to come. Getting to heaven does not depend on these. And when we rely on our decisions for eternal matters, we are worshiping the idol of our will. Trust instead in God.

◇◇◇◇

Letter 54

You might be wondering at this point if we just trust in faith itself. Well, Jesus does not want us to have just any old kind of faith. He wants us to trust in Him. So that we might trust in Him, He gives us His Word in which He tells us all sorts of things that He has done for us. He lived for us. He did miracles that teach us all sorts of things about Him. He died for us. He rose again to open the gates of heaven for us. It's not about faith; it's about Jesus.

And the questions we ask should not be about faith. We should not agonize over whether our faith is strong enough or sincere enough, heartfelt enough or active enough. We should not really analyze faith at all. Instead, we should fix our eyes on Jesus.

Is your faith strong enough? I don't know. Is mine? I really doubt it sometimes. But Jesus is strong. He rose from the dead. I trust Him. You can trust Him too.

Is your faith sincere enough? I don't know. I don't think anyone is sufficiently sincere at all times. I know myself, and I am not particularly sincere. But Jesus was very sincere when He died for you, and that is all the sincerity you need.

Is your faith heartfelt enough? I don't even know what that means. I know that my faith is often not felt, and that my heart is often heavy or distracted. But I also know that Jesus took my heaviness and my distractions upon Himself. And that is enough for me.

Is your faith active enough? Do you pray without ceasing and devote every minute of every day to loving God and serving those around you? Do you act every day all day as though the most important thing in your life is God? No, you don't. No one has faith like that. That's why you need Jesus. That's why Jesus came. He forgives us our lack of active faith. What makes faith valuable, as I said about fifteen letters ago (Letter 39), is that faith *holds* to Jesus. God wants us to trust in Jesus and not in our own faith.

A famous Early American Puritan preacher by the name of Jonathan Edwards made an unfortunate contribution to American religious thinking, and we have been suffering ever since. He lived in the early eighteenth century and was the first influential American to insist that faith must be evaluated and analyzed psychologically so as to determine its truth and sincerity. His goal was that the people have true faith, but he did not understand how we determine whether faith is true. So instead of pointing people to Jesus and to the Word of the Gospel, he pointed people to their own faith. He told the people that their certainty came from the feelings of faith, the choices of faith, the struggles of faith, the anguish of faith, or the heartfelt sincerity of faith. Edwards encouraged a psychological understanding of faith rather than a Gospel understanding of faith. Ever since then, Americans have had this obsession with faith rather than with the object of faith—Jesus and His Word.

So, Christians, such as you and I, are constantly tempted to doubt our Savior because our faith is not up to snuff. Jesus did not come so that we could sit and indulge ourselves in self-analysis. He came to take our thoughts away from ourselves and to place these thoughts on Him, who truly and most sincerely lived and died for you.

Faith can be the worst idol of all if it replaces Jesus as the focus of our attention.

◇◇◇◇

The Faith That Jesus Commends: The Centurion

Letter 55

There are a few people in the Bible whom Jesus commends for their faith. So let's look at three stories and see what true faith really is. Luke 7 tells us the story of a centurion who had a sick servant. The Jewish elders came to Jesus and said that Jesus should do what the centurion wanted because he deserved it. (Apparently the centurion had done some generous things for the Jews of his community.) So these Jewish advocates believed in a type of *quid pro quo* view of our relationship with God. You do your part, and we will do our part. The centurion did generous things for us; now we should heal his servant.

This is how many people view faith. They think that God has done His part by sending His Son for us, and we do our part by having a lively and heartfelt faith in Jesus. Of course, since Jesus did so much for us, our faith has to be particularly strong and vibrant—this is what we do for Him in return. Usually, the type of person who advocates this view is someone particularly pleased with his or her own faith.

But God is not someone with whom you negotiate. God, in fact, not only did His part by placing us in this world but He sent Jesus to do our part by redeeming us through His life and death. Christians do not offer their faith to God to impress Him.

The centurion, when he noticed that Jesus was coming to his house, quickly sent friends to say to Jesus, "Lord, do not trouble Yourself, for I am not worthy to have You come under my roof" (v. 6). He was clearly nervous that Jesus would actually think that he felt he deserved something. At the end of the story, Jesus commends that man's great faith. So it is obvious that Jesus commends the type of faith that is able to say, "I don't deserve anything."

That's what true Christians learn to say. "Lord, I really don't deserve anything. And especially my faith does not deserve anything. My faith is worthless and paltry and completely nothing." Paul says something similar in 1 Corinthians: "God chose what is foolish in the world to shame the wise; God chose what is weak in the world to shame the strong; God chose what is low and despised in the world, even things that are not, to bring to nothing things that are, so that no human being might boast in the presence of God" (1:27–29). Since God chose foolish, weak, and lowly things, I guess that makes us qualified, Lloyd. And if your faith is not adequate, then welcome to the club of foolish, weak, lowly people whom God calls His Church.

The centurion sent word to Jesus: "I am not worthy to have You come under my roof. Therefore I did not presume to come to You. But say the word, and let my servant be healed." Now there is a faith worth copying. There is no mention of the man's struggle, his sentiments, his strength of conviction, his feelings, or anything that would describe faith. He simply trusted that Jesus could speak the word and heal.

That is the faith that Jesus commended, "I tell you, not even in Israel have I found such faith" (v. 9).

What God wants in faith is for us to listen to and trust the strength of His Word. I doubt if the centurion even thought about his faith. He was too busy thinking about the promises and word of Jesus. He had great faith.

◇◇◇◇

The Faith That Jesus Commends: The Sinful Woman

Letter 56

In Luke 7 there is another story of a woman whom Jesus commends for her faith. This is the sinful woman, probably an adulteress, who came and washed the feet of Jesus. She was incredibly devout toward Him, anointing His feet with oil, kissing His feet, and wiping His tear-drenched feet with her hair.

People complained that Jesus was allowing a woman with a scandalous reputation to touch Him. So Jesus told a story in which a moneylender forgave two men their debts. One owed a huge amount of money and the other a rather modest amount. Who would love the moneylender more? The obvious and correct answer is that the person who is forgiven more loves more. Then Jesus pointed out the great love of the sinful woman who anointed Him and concluded that the ones who have the most commendable faith are those who have been forgiven the most. Now think about this, Lloyd. This would suggest that the most important qualification for the favor of God is that we are scandalous sinners. I would expect that you and I qualify.

Jesus said to the woman, "Your faith has saved you; go in peace" (Luke 7:50). I imagine that anyone would love to hear these words from Jesus, and you do hear these words in church every Sunday. You go to church, confess your sins, and the pastor forgives you in the name of Jesus. He does not ask you to analyze the strength of your faith, but the size of your sins, believing that His grace is bigger than your offenses. Then you go to the Lord's Supper and the pastor gives you the body and blood of Jesus for the forgiveness of your sins. You are not asked to agonize over your sins or to feel the presence of God. You are told that you are eating with your mouth the body and blood of Jesus. At the end of the service the pastor speaks the Benediction, which includes the words, "The Lord . . . give you peace." Well, consider that. You receive the forgiveness of sins and are told to go in peace. It is exactly the same as the woman in our story (Luke 7:36–50). She is left with the word from Christ, "Your sins are forgiven. . . . Your faith has saved you; go in peace."

How does your faith save you? It trusts Jesus. Jesus gives two judgments, and true faith accepts them both. We believe the judgment of Christ that we have many sins. We believe the judgment of Jesus: "Your sins are forgiven."

These two judgments of Jesus, incidentally, are called the Law and the promise. His Law says we are egregious sinners, and His promise says, "I forgive you." The greater the sin, the greater the forgiveness; and the greater the forgiveness, the more the commendation.

If you wonder about your faith, then ask yourself three questions: Am I a sinner? Have I been forgiven by Jesus through His death on the cross? Has He spoken His word of forgiveness to me? Yes, Yes, Yes. So you have a good faith. Faith is nothing more than the ability to see your sin in God's Law and to see your Savior in His promises.

The Faith That Jesus Commends: The Canaanite Woman

Letter 57

No story in the Bible demonstrates the value of faith more dramatically than the story of the Canaanite woman in Matthew 15. A woman cries out to Jesus, asking Him to heal her daughter. "Have mercy on me, O Lord, Son of David" (v. 22). She is so obnoxious that the disciples beg Jesus to get rid of her. Jesus says to her, "I was sent only to the lost sheep of the house of Israel" (v. 24). She continues to ask for help. Finally, He says, "It is not right to take the children's bread and throw it to the dogs" (v. 26). She replies, "Yes, Lord, yet even the dogs eat the crumbs that fall from their masters' table" (v. 27). Then Jesus expresses amazement at the greatness of her faith and heals her daughter. So what is so awesome about this woman's faith?

I will tell you first, Lloyd, what was *not* awesome about her faith. Never is it mentioned that she even thought about her own faith. Never is it mentioned that she agonized over the sincerity of faith. Never is it mentioned that she exercised her will in the matter or made any decisions or choices. Never is she said to have been dedicated or on fire for Jesus. Rather her faith was precious precisely because of whom she trusted and what she knew.

First, she called Jesus "Lord." Then she called Him the "Son of David." So she knew that Jesus was God and that He had come into the world as the promised Heir of David, who would be a Shepherd for His people and even die for them. She had heard the Word and believed it.

Second, she was willing to admit her sin. "Yes, I'm a dog. I can easily be a dog if it means that I can get a couple of scraps." Never does she boast or act better than she is. Never does she lecture Jesus on His manners, even though He appeared a bit rude. Never does she ask to be rewarded for her faith. She was willing to admit her unworthiness. She was every bit like those Lutherans who go to church on Sunday and say, "I, a poor, miserable sinner, confess unto You all my sins and iniquities with which I have ever offended You." There is no pride here. There is nothing in her or in her faith that deserves any attention.

Third, she trusts that God has grace for her. "Yes, Lord, yet even the dogs eat the crumbs." She understood grace. Grace, actually, never comes in crumbs. It always comes in huge chunks. God never forgives halfway or heals halfway. His promises are always more than we can possibly need or even anticipate. True faith trusts that there is enough of God's extravagant love to go around to all of us. Faith grabs and holds and will not let go.

Jesus says, "Great is your faith!" (Matthew 15:28), and He is commending all who are willing to say, "I do not deserve." He is commending all who know who He is, and especially He is commending all who want even the smallest scrap of mercy.

These three examples of people whose faith was commended by Jesus ought to teach us that even the lowliest Christian with the smallest and weakest faith is wonderfully blessed. If you know that you are nothing, that you deserve nothing, that Jesus accepts you by grace, that He is your God and the Son of David, that He willingly forgives sins no matter how many, that He has grace enough for all—if you believe all that, then you are to be commended no less than these faithful people of the Bible.

I was able to visit Lloyd again in March of 2007. It was a short but precious visit as we were able to talk for a couple of hours. He had continued to go to church, which, of course, thrilled the entire family, and he was eager to talk about Christian matters.

Propitiously, he had recently read the account of the rich young man in Matthew 19 who was told by Jesus to give all he had to the poor and follow the Lord. Lloyd was struggling with the story. Blessed with a very sensitive conscience, he confessed that he saw no way in which he could live up to God's standards as he had come to understand them. Now, besides the guilt effected by the Ten Commandments, he also felt a bit guilty for not embracing the idea that he should part with all of his money in deference to the poor. Lloyd had been thrifty enough over his many years to save a not-so-modest nest egg. Now, he was actually thinking of giving it away so as to gain eternal life, as if heaven could have been purchased with his meager savings.

I wasn't sure whether or not he was completely serious, but I felt it my duty to disabuse him of such a thought. I certainly did not want to have to explain to his daughters that my evangelistic efforts had resulted in the complete loss of their inheritance. More important, I had spent quite a few weeks trying to explain to Lloyd that the price for his salvation had already been paid.

So, we talked about the rich young man and there followed one of those conversations that are all too rare. I was able to dialogue with a man I loved who truly wanted to understand Jesus and His Gospel. I've learned over the years not to expect or demand an immediate faith confession to the things I say about Christ. We just talked. We were both very interested in what the other said. We talked about Jesus.

The next morning I had breakfast with Lloyd and three of his daughters. I drove off at about noon. It was the last time I saw Lloyd alive.

◇◇◇◇

The Second-Most Important Teaching of the Bible

Letter 58

Lloyd, our conversation led us to a great story in the book of Matthew—the story of the rich young man from Matthew 19. I must say that you have understood this story remarkably well.

In this story you see very clearly the second-most important teaching of the Bible and its purpose. Here, God teaches us His Law. (For the most important teaching of the Bible you will have to wait a couple of days.) Look at this man who comes to Jesus. In his own eyes he has never sinned. He has kept all of the Commandments since his youth. He is truly full of himself. So Jesus has to empty the man of himself. People so confident in themselves are unfit for the kingdom of heaven.

I teach this story to our young confirmands every year, and most of them think that Jesus is trying to teach us that generosity is the way to heaven. Obviously, generosity is a virtue commended by God, but it is not what saves us. The primary point of the story is not that we need to be generous.

Rather, and you seemed to grasp this, Lloyd, Jesus wants us to realize that there is nothing we can do to gain life. Keeping the Commandments will not accomplish life for us. That's why Jesus did not argue with the guy about whether he truly had obeyed. Instead, He gave him one more thing to do—the thing He knew the man could not do.

I always ask the kids, "What would Jesus have said if the young man had gone out and given everything he had to the poor and followed Jesus?" Most of them think that the rich young man would then have been able to go to heaven. But that is not what Jesus was teaching. Every once in a while someone in my class says, "He would have given him something else to do. And Jesus would have kept giving him things to do until the man admitted that he had failed." That is the lesson of the story. And that, Lloyd, is what you understood. The Law of God is always one more thing to do. It tells us to do and do and do until we simply get depressed about all there is to do.

People who think they have actually kept God's Law are lying to themselves. Either they have too high an estimate of themselves or too low an estimate of God's Law. Those with the first problem need to be knocked down by God. Those with the second problem need the same but in a different way. The way in which God knocks us down will be the topic of my next two letters.

The Law Knocks Us Down: Part One

Letter 59

All people tend toward the arrogance of the rich young man. We read the Law of God and say, "I can do that." Of course it honors God to follow His commands. But it dishonors God to think that we actually have done so perfectly.

I knew a man in college who ran the bookstore. He actually claimed that he had not sinned against God consciously for three years. He knew the Ten Commandments. He knew Matthew 5, where Jesus says that hate, rage, lust, and selfishness are sins punishable by hell. And this man had kept these laws; or so he thought. One day my friends and I were arguing with him, and one of my friends said, "Have you sold everything and given it to the poor?" Obviously the man had not done that. He owned a car and a house. (I think he even owned a boat.) Yet he answered, "Yes." I remember being amazed at the lie he was speaking. And I stopped being angry with him and started being sad for him. I realized that he was forced to think such lies because he could not face the reality that he was truly a sinner.

Our culture is full of the notion that we are actually pretty good people. Think of some of the songs that are popular. From *The Sound of Music* we hear that we deserve good things because we ourselves did good things in our youth and childhood. It's as if we simply are worthy of all the good we get. Or think of the Cavaliers' song "Last Kiss" where we sing that if we want to get to heaven to see our departed loved ones when we die, then we got to be good. The sentiment is based on the prevailing notion that heaven is within our grasp if we simply are good enough. It's just like saying, "All these have I kept even from my youth."

In the catechism, it says that the Law has three functions or purposes. One is to restrain people. Another is to be a guide: the Law informs us as to what is right and wrong. The most important function of the Law is so that we can have a theological mirror; the Law shows us our sin.

> It was a false, misleading dream
> That God His Law had given
> That sinners could themselves redeem
> And by their works gain heaven.
> The Law is but a mirror bright
> To bring the inbred sin to light
> That lurks within our nature. (*LSB* 555:3)

When I hear the Law, I ought to wince. The Law shows me my sin. Honor your parents? I never did that too well. Thou shalt not kill? Well, I have certainly hurt people, and some badly and on purpose. Thou shalt not commit adultery? The Bible says that divorce is adultery, so that makes me guilty. Don't bear false witness? I suppose I have done my share of gossiping. And these are the easy ones. Honor the Sabbath? That means hold His Word as high as heaven. I have not done that. Have no others gods? I hope that all my letters on "American Idol" have shown the difficulty of obeying that commandment. Each of the Ten Commandments indicts me. I read them and weep. I wince because I know I'm guilty. And there are all sorts of other commands in the Scriptures that make me a sinner if I can only learn to be honest.

The Law is a mirror. It makes us lower our estimate of ourselves as we stand before the bar of God's justice. It knocks us down.

◇◇◇◇

The Law Knocks Us Down: Part Two

Letter 60

It is so unpleasant to stand before God acknowledging our guilt that people have a couple of built-in ways of lying to themselves so as to avoid guilt. One is to overestimate ourselves. That was the topic of the previous letter. The second is to underestimate God's Law. And this is far more popular today than we may realize.

The most popular way in which we, as a culture, have underestimated God's Law is simply to change it so that it fits our behavior. That way we don't have to deal with our own guilt.

Have you noticed that the moral standards of our culture seem to have eroded over the last forty years? A generation ago public prayers were in the name of Jesus and no one would have dreamt of being sworn into public office by invoking the Qur'an. I remember going to church on Sunday and having to drive slowly because of all the cars. That hasn't happened lately. Honoring God on His day is a thing of the past. You would never have had children's sporting events scheduled on Sunday a generation ago. Today, it is a common thing. It used to be that swearing and vulgar language was inappropriate in public. Now, you hear it all the time. It used to be wrong to live together before marriage. Now, it is perfectly acceptable behavior according to our culture. It used to be that modesty was a cherished commodity. No more. It used to be that certain types of sexual behavior were considered morally taboo. Now very little is wrong.

The standards of our society have changed. We no longer have the same definition of right and wrong that we did forty years ago when I graduated from high school. I am convinced that the reason for this is primarily theological. Why?

I believe that the people of our culture (Western civilization) have been open to a redefinition of right and wrong because morally we have failed, at least by God's standards. And rather than admit that we have fallen short of God's expectations—His Law—we simply have deluded ourselves into thinking that the Law has changed. Instead of learning to repent, we have changed the rules so that repentance is unnecessary.

When we lived in North Dakota, my son Klemet used to play in our unfinished basement. He would take a damp tennis ball and throw it against a target that he had drawn on the concrete wall. The damp ball would make a mark and he could see how close to the bull's eye he was able to come. One day, he excitedly asked me to come and see what he had done. Amazingly, he had thrown the ball only once, and the ball had found itself in the middle of the target. I was praising him profusely when he began to laugh. It turns out that he had played a little trick on me. He had reversed the order of things by first throwing the ball and then drawing the target around it. We both laughed at his harmless ruse.

This type of deception is fine when it comes to throwing tennis balls against the wall, but we tend to do the same thing morally. We alter the Law to fit our behavior in order to cope with its demands. And this way there is no need for repentance and, worse yet, no need of forgiveness. Jesus also has been redefined.

God does not agree with these changes in our definition of right and wrong. And though it may be easier for us to be self-congratulatory about our behavior under the current moral codes of our culture, this code is not the benchmark against which God judges us. He does not draw the target after the ball has been thrown.

◇◇◇◇

The Law Knocks Us Down: Part Three

The Primary Offense

Letter 61

Luther called the Law "God's alien work." It just smashes us and destroys us. It is not fun to speak and less fun to hear. I speak it with great reluctance both because I do not want to seem disrespectful and also because it may seem imprudent to speak harshly to someone struggling in their faith. I want very much to speak a different and happier word of God to you, but I must speak the Law first. Jesus spoke harshly to the rich young man and the intent was to destroy the young man's sense of self-worth. Please forgive me if these letters are harsh; it's because they are "alien."

So, to continue from last time, our abilities are less than we like to think. And the Law of God is much more difficult than we might assume. What a deadly combination. To compound matters, something happened to the entire human race long ago that renders us unable even to begin a process of getting back to God. I speak of the original sin—when Adam and Eve ate the fruit in the garden.

I'm sure, Lloyd, that you are familiar with the story. Adam and Eve ate fruit from the forbidden tree because they thought that God had withheld something from them (Genesis 3). They saw that the fruit was pleasing. They ate. Luther compared the tree to an altar: It was God's place. It was placed in the garden to give people an opportunity to treat God holy by treating His tree holy.

The effect of that one sin is profound and far-reaching. Not only did the trespass make Adam and Eve sinners, it made all of their descendants sinners. God says, "Just as sin came into the world through one man, and death through sin, and so death spread to all men because all sinned. . . . Many died through one man's trespass. . . . One trespass led to condemnation for all men. . . . By the one man's disobedience the many were made sinners" (Romans 5:12, 15, 18, 19). That means that God has counted the guilt of our first parents against you and me. The psalmist says, "Behold, I was brought forth in iniquity, and in sin did my mother conceive me" (Psalm 51:5). Here again we learn that we are sinful even before we have had the opportunity to do anything. We are afflicted with that first sin—the original sin.

Are we sinful because we sin or do we sin because we are sinful? Common sense might suggest that we really can't be called sinful until we have actually done something wrong. But the Scriptures have more authority than our common sense, and they teach the opposite. We are born with a sinful nature, sinful tendencies, and even guilt. God has held us guilty for the sins of others. We are guilty with Adam's sin. So the answer to the question is: We sin because we are sinful.

Our sinful actions reflect something more deadly than the actions themselves. We are by nature sinful and corrupt. So corrupt, in fact, is our condition, that we are capable of nothing at all when it comes to our relationship with God. We can't earn, seek, find, or strive after His good favor. God's good favor is given. God saves us by grace, by His Word and Sacraments.

You mentioned to me, Lloyd, that you are troubled when you go to the Lord's Supper because you do not believe that you are worthy. I would suggest that you are right—you are not worthy. Your condition is too corrupt and your faith too weak for you to think yourself worthy. Both the story of the rich young lawyer and your highly functional conscience have told you that you are unworthy, and they are both correct. It seems apparent that your conscience and your sense of unworthiness are the effect of the natural, inherited guilt and corruption that troubles you and the whole human race. It is not unusual to feel unworthy or to think that your faith is not adequate. If our worthiness depended on our performance, or our conscience, or even our faith, none would be worthy. So your feelings at the altar are understandable. But there is an antidote that I will tell you about soon.

◇◇◇◇

The Law Knocks Us Down: Part Four

God's Anger

 Letter 62

The Law of God is impossibly difficult. We are unable to obey it. And, to make matters even worse, the consequences of this tragedy are overwhelmingly awful. You can find these consequences in Ephesians 2:1–3.

- Our condition is dire. We are dead in our sins. There is no possibility to be a spiritual Horatio Alger and pick ourselves up by the bootstraps.
- We are under the control of the devil when it comes to the way we relate to God. We naturally tend to follow his prodding and enticements just like Adam and Eve.
- We are self-centered. We want to please our flesh, which is ourselves. It's all about me and what I want.
- Most formidably, we are children of wrath. That means that we tend to function from the posture of anger and that we bring upon ourselves God's anger in return.

Now, I know that it is extremely unpopular today to depict God as angry. It's also unpopular to consider people sinful or even flawed. And it's especially unpopular to teach God's Law in all its severity. So we need to get past being popular and face some grim realities. God is angry. "The wrath of God is revealed from heaven against all ungodliness and unrighteousness of men" (Romans 1:18). "I the Lord your God am a jealous God, visiting the iniquity of the fathers on the children to the third and the fourth generation of those who hate Me" (Exodus 20:5). "You are not a God who delights in wickedness; evil may not dwell with You. The boastful shall not stand before Your eyes; You hate all evildoers" (Psalm 5:4–5). Ouch! These words are hard to accept and impossible to tone down. Yet here they are.

Consider what God said to the children of Israel when they entered the Promised Land:

> The LORD your God is a consuming fire, a jealous God. When you father children and children's children, and have grown old in the land, if you act corruptly by making a carved image in the form of anything, and by doing what is evil in the sight of the LORD your God, so as to provoke Him to anger, I call heaven and earth to witness against you today, that you will soon utterly perish from the land that you are going over the Jordan to possess. You will not live long in it, but will be utterly destroyed. (Deuteronomy 4:24–26)

These words apply to us as well, and they ought to make us truly afraid of God. We should be desperate for another way into His good graces than by our own efforts.

Why does God speak this way? Because it is true and because He wants to warn us even of Himself. He knows His own justice, and He knows that He cannot deny this justice. He knows His own holiness, and this cannot be transgressed. Yet He loves us and wants to have fellowship with us. He wants to be near us and have us with Him. So He warns us of what most certainly will happen if we prefer idols to our Creator and if we choose our own interests above God's. And then God offers us an alternative to the deadly consequences of our sin. He provides a word of something new and radically different from His Law, which exposes our guilt and sin and reveals His anger and justice. Luther calls this new word God speaks to us "God's Proper work."

◇◇◇◇

The Gospel

Letter 63

God understands the harshness of His Law. He is a little like you, Lloyd. Jan tells me that you were forced at times to discipline your daughters. But she insists that you did not particularly enjoy it when you had to chide or rebuke or scold. She is convinced that you did it out of love, because, though painful, it was necessary. And she is positive that you much preferred more kindly and winsome expressions of affection.

So it is with God. He does not enjoy speaking His Law to us. He knows that it knocks us down and crushes us. He does not relish seeing the people whom He created and whom He sustains reeling like drunken college kids under the dizzying barrage of His commands. He knows that His Law does not and has never brought out the best in His people.

Yet He must speak it. We are all like that rich young lawyer. We must hear the expectations of our God and concede our inability to realize them before we can hear God's proper and gracious Word. And once God has crushed us and made us realize our guilt, He has an altogether different message: "I forgive you."

He says, "I forgive you. I sent My Son to carry in Himself your sins. Your sins—offenses against My righteousness and exposed by My Law; your sins—inherited from your first parents along with the guilt they incurred; your sins—which trouble your conscience and make you feel unworthy. Your sins have been placed upon My Son, Jesus Christ, and He has been punished by Me for what you and your parents did wrong. I no longer hold you accountable for your own offenses. I have held Christ accountable. I no longer feel anger against you. I was angry with Christ instead. I forgive you."

That little message, which is the core and fundamental message of Jesus, is very good news. It is Gospel.

We use the word *forgive* much more loosely than God does. When I forgive someone, it means that I will overlook his or her bad behavior. Or it might mean that I will not be angry with someone for a thing that he did. Sometimes to forgive, for me, means that I will try to forget. But forgetting offenses is psychologically very difficult and usually takes place only in time and only when the consequences of the offense diminish. God's forgiveness is greater than that.

Jan had informed me a couple of days earlier that her dad was still struggling with miracles. This time, it was not precisely that he questioned their possibility or even their historicity. Rather, he was curious as to precisely what scientific or natural law was suspended and in what way in order for the effects of a miracle to occur. Precisely how had God done a miracle? So I decided to go back to the beginning briefly, treading some old ground with Lloyd and trying to lead to the consideration of a more personal miracle in his life.

Analyzing Miracles

Letter 64

These letters to you, Lloyd, have forced me to think about miracles more intently and analytically than I had before. I suppose I owe you a debt of thanks for that. I think that Christians have two ways of looking at miracles and believing them.

The first way is a presentation of the data to someone who is scientifically skeptical in an attempt to satisfy even the most rigorous scrutiny. That's what I did when I wrote to you last summer. I wrote about the historical and scientific evidence for the truthfulness of miracles in the Bible. I talked about how any miracle claim must be both falsifiable and verifiable. That's why the virgin birth is a difficult miracle, because it is almost impossible to verify or falsify. The resurrection, on the other hand, is open to verification and falsification. It is presented so as to invite historical and scientific scrutiny. This first approach to miracles does not talk about faith until the facts are clearly established. Faith must be based on historical facts, because the entire Christian faith is predicated upon the belief that God has entered our history in Christ and has done some remarkable things in our world that were observed and recorded by reliable eyewitnesses.

There is a second approach to miracles that I will now present. It begins with fear of God, moves to confidence in the Gospel, and then works back to an analysis of the claims of the Bible. Think about it. Most people don't make a thorough investigation of the historical reliability of the witnesses and a painstaking analysis of the miracles and then choose the most sensible way of believing. Most Christians feel their sin so acutely that they are open and ready to hear of some relief for the guilt. When they hear that God, in Christ, has provided a way to be free from guilt, they are ready to listen. When people hear that there is a way to have a pleasant and pleasing relationship with God, they are eager to have it through the Gospel of Jesus. All this happens before the person thinks through all the issues surrounding the possibility and provability of miracles.

I think that's the way you are, Lloyd. You know deep down that you are sinful before God. You know that you have not met His just demands. That's why you have a sense of fear and foreboding when you go to the Lord's Supper. How can you presume to come before His presence and expect a blessing when you are so frail and sinful—when your failings and shortcomings are so apparent? God is not fooled into thinking that we actually deserve to come before Him. If you stopped to consider this, you would have to conclude that everyone else who approaches the altar is just as sinful and equally unworthy. How could anyone approach God with anything but fear?

We are like Manoah, the father of Samson, who, when he realized that he had been conversing with the Lord, was totally convinced that he was going to die (Judges 13:22). We are like the shepherds who, when in the presence of the glory of the Lord, could do nothing more than be "filled with great fear" (Luke 2:9). That is why one of God's favorite words to sinners is precisely what He is saying in the Sacrament of the Altar: "Don't be afraid." He said it to Manoah and to the shepherds. He said it to Jairus immediately before raising his daughter from the dead (Mark 5:36). And especially He says it to you, Lloyd. He does not speak to you in scientific jargon hoping to convince you of the scientific reliability of the miracle accounts. Rather, He says, "I see that you are afraid. Don't be. I am here not to hurt you but to heal you."

God is not your science teacher or your history instructor. He is your Father. He speaks to you like a father. He says, "Here, take this. This is Christ's body. Here, take this. It's His blood. This is good for you. It will make things better. It is shed to forgive your sins." Would a father ever give something to his son which is harmful or which is not precisely what he says? Does God give anything but good to you?

◇◇◇◇

FAITH IN THE BLOOD

Letter 65

Skeptics try to disprove God's miracles. Believers simply trust in Him.

You have received into your mouth the body of Christ, which is in the bread. You have drunk His blood, which is in the wine. You have God's eternal and gracious promise that through this body and blood you are delivered from the worthlessness that is so apparent. Instead of sorrow, you are clothed with gladness. "Weeping may tarry for the night, but joy comes with the morning" (Psalm 30:5). God feeds you in such a manner—as a father provides food for his children.

So, where does faith come in? Faith trusts that the body and blood forgive our sins and make us worthy before God.

Do you remember the Passover meal that I recounted in Letter 33? The angel of death was going to kill everyone without blood on their door (Exodus 12). So those who trusted in the promises of God took the blood and placed in on the door. The angel then passed over their homes and they were delivered. Luther wrote an Easter hymn in which he said,

> Here our true Paschal Lamb we see,
> Whom God so freely gave us;
> He died on the accursèd tree—
> So strong His love—to save us.
> See, His blood now marks our door;
> Faith points to it; death passes o'er,
> And Satan cannot harm us.
> Allelulia! (*LSB* 458:5)

Faith says to God: Look, there is the blood on the door of my body and in my mouth. And, dear Father, You put it there. You told me to take the blood. More, You put it in my mouth. And You promised that those with the blood of Jesus in their mouths would not have to be afraid. So, dear Father, I am not afraid.

Luther once said that we should rub God's nose in His promises. So, Lloyd, rub. Tell God that He has promised. Be like a little child and remind your Father that He must keep His word to you. Children do not argue the reasonableness or the empirical likelihood of their father's promises. They simply remind him, "But, Dad, you promised."

"Take, eat; this is My body. . . . Drink of it, all of you, for this is My blood of the covenant, which is poured out for many for the forgiveness of sins" (Matthew 26:26–28).

These are promises. They are God's Word. They cannot lie, no matter who opposes them. They are the last will and testament of Christ the Lord. They are literally true and legally binding upon Him. They are for you. And this precious meal is a miracle.

◇◇◇◇

If God Can Do One Miracle . . .

Letter 66

Now, Lloyd, the body of our Lord in the Sacrament came from somewhere. It is the body of Christ that carried your sins to the cross. That blood is the blood of the Lamb of God, who hung on the cross and who takes away the sins of the world.

If God can feed you with such wonderful food, can't He do more? And if this is indeed a wonderful food, then the body and blood of Jesus are not rotting in some grave near Jerusalem. If the Sacrament of the Altar is anything, it is a testimony to the real life, death, and resurrection of Jesus, who loved you and gave Himself for you.

Every time we go to the Sacrament, we are reminded of what Paul says: "As often as you eat this bread and drink this cup, you proclaim the Lord's death until He comes" (1 Corinthians 11:26). Notice that we celebrate "until He comes." Jesus is still alive. He is coming back. He must have been raised.

You told me, Lloyd, that you feel a sense of unworthiness before you go to the Sacrament. That seems pretty natural. In the presence of Christ you sense your own smallness. But for those feelings to be true—and I believe they are true—then the Lord's Supper must be something more than bread and wine. Holy Communion must be important in order for you to feel unworthy before it. It must be a miracle based upon a greater miracle—the resurrection of Jesus.

If Christ is raised, then a whole host of other biblical claims are also true. I mentioned some of them in Letter 10. If Christ is raised, then the Bible is true, our faith is valid, and you, too, will rise from the dead. All these wonderful biblical Gospel truths depend on the resurrection.

And there is one more truth. If the resurrection is true, then God has body and blood to feed us, and grace to spare. If the resurrection is true, then the miracle of eating and drinking His body and blood for the forgiveness of sins ought not be so daunting to believe.

There is a deep yearning within each human heart for something greater than what we have. Jesus is that something. And when you taste Him in the Supper, then the Holy Spirit works in you to give and build your faith. If you keep eating and drinking and eating and drinking, that Spirit convinces you of something. What?

He convinces you of Jesus.

You cannot hear the words over and over again, "Given for you. Shed for you," without embracing the miracle of forgiveness through Christ's death and resurrection. You cannot taste the body and blood week in and week out without God placing deep within you the unassailable conviction that you are intimately connected to Him and His saving grace.

As Christ was raised, so you, through sharing in His death by the Sacrament, are raised from the death of doubt to the life of certainty in His body and blood.

And that is another miracle.

◇◇◇◇

Miracles Are Objective

Letter 67

Most of us accept the biblical miracles initially not because we have done an objective study of them. Rather, we accept them because we trust our Father in heaven and believe that He wants to bless us. We believe the miracles because we have faith in God's grace. Habitual partaking of Christ's body and blood in the Lord's Supper tends to create certainty in the miracles. But, that doesn't mean that you need faith to be able to know that a miracle has occurred. Miracles are obvious to everyone except to those whose convictions or needs will not allow them to see the truth.

Now, someone might claim that the miracle of the Lord's Supper is true only in the minds of those who are devoted to Jesus. Someone might say that objective, dispassionate observers would conclude that the miracles are only true in our hearts but not in reality. It is claimed that only believers see the miracle.

But this seems rather silly to me. The soldiers who lied about the disciples stealing the body of Jesus were "scientifically" convinced that the body was gone. They knew Jesus had been raised; they just preferred money to acknowledging the truth (Matthew 28:11–15). The Jewish leaders who hated Jesus knew that Lazarus had been raised from the dead. They were so convinced that He had been raised, that they were determined to kill Him again if they could (John 12:9–11). It seems to me that the reason they questioned and denied the miracles publicly (for they certainly believed them privately) is that they were not at all dispassionate and objective.

Christians haven't lost their scientific objectivity—unbelievers have. Those who hated Jesus were unable to look at the miracle claims without also wondering how it would affect them financially or in regard to their political or churchly power. John says as much when he reveals the true motives of those who did not accept the truth of miracles. "What are we to do?" they asked. "This man performs many signs. If we let Him go on like this, everyone will believe in Him, and the Romans will come and take away both our place and our nation" (John 11:47–48). The point is that those who did not publicly acknowledge the miracles still knew they happened. They denied them out of greed and self-interest. Those that did not confess faith in the miracle of the resurrection were the real anti-scientists.

Still, the resurrection miracles alone did not engender faith in the detractors of Christ. Faith does not come by miracles. Rather, faith comes from hearing the Word of God (Romans 10:17).

Lloyd, if you were convinced that the miracle of the resurrection occurred and that was all, then you would be no different than the Jews who killed Jesus or the soldiers who lied about the circumstances of His resurrection. Faith is more than a conviction that the miracles occurred. It is confidence that God blesses you through the miracles. And you don't need to see, feel, or experience the miracles for this to occur. Rather, eat the body, drink the blood, hear the Word, and recall your Baptism. Listen to God speak forgiveness over and over again. Be a child to your Father and pay attention to Him as He speaks promises to you.

At this point in my correspondence I was made aware that the letters were being passed around to other family members. With others overhearing our conversation, I decided to simply teach some theology based on the Creed.

The Apostles' Creed: First Article

Letter 68

Just prior to my visit last spring, I sent you Martin Luther's Small Catechism. The catechism has six parts: Ten Commandments, Apostles' Creed, Lord's Prayer, Baptism, Confession and Absolution, and Holy Communion. These are often called the six chief parts of the Christian faith since just about everything a Christian knows and practices is contained in these six parts.

I thought it might be helpful, through these letters, to explain one of the six parts since many of the questions you have seem to center in that part of the catechism. I am speaking of the Apostles' Creed, which you probably hear often in church.

The creed wasn't actually formulated by Jesus' apostles; it was developed very early in the Church's life and is universally believed and known to be the teaching of the Twelve and of Jesus. It has been used as the basis of instructing new Christians as they prepare for Baptism. Most Christians learn its meaning as they prepare to receive the Lord's Supper for the first time. With the exception of certain fringe groups, every Christian church body for the last 1,700 years has accepted the Apostles' Creed as a truthful expression of God's Word. So what does it mean?

The Creed is best analyzed when divided into three parts (or articles)—each one corresponding to one of the persons of the Trinity. Typically, we start with a look at God the Father, who created heaven and earth. But even this division in the Creed could be a bit misleading, for it might give the impression that neither the Son nor the Holy Spirit had anything to do with the creation of the world. Actually, they did! Genesis says that the Spirit was hovering over the waters (1:2). The Spirit has often been called “Creator Spirit” because He created the world and us just as much as the Father did.

The Bible also tells us that Jesus created the world. “All things were made through Him, and without Him was not any thing made that was made” (John 1:3). We owe a debt of thanks to God—Father, Son, and Holy Spirit—for the beautiful world in which we live. And we owe the triune God thanks also for the manner in which this world is preserved and cared for.

The Bible teaches that God created the world all by Himself without any help from anyone or anything else.

Unfortunately, the biblical account of creation is challenged by much of the scientific community today. So let me talk about the First Article of the Creed and why it is both biblically and scientifically defensible.

Letter 69

The Bible says that God created the world in six days, and on the seventh day He rested. That suggests the world was created in a very short period of time. But many scientists claim the world came into being over a process that was guided by chance and that took place over billions of years.

I believe this little controversy could easily be resolved if scientists would understand one aspect of what Christians are saying. Christians claim, on the basis of the Bible, that God created a fully functional world in six days.

When scientists see the world and examine it, they theorize that mountains are billions of years old because they are rounded. They think that deep valleys are millions of years old because they are wind blown. They think that birds came from eggs and that these eggs took a certain amount of time to hatch. They see trees and count rings to determine their age. They look at men and women and surmise their age by examining them.

But God did not merely make acorns; He made fully-grown oak trees. He did not only create eggs; He created chickens. In the Garden of Eden, God did not make a fetus; He created a fully-grown man. God did not merely create shorelines; He created shorelines with rounded rocks on them that had the appearance of being pounded by the water for centuries. He did not only create the Rocky Mountains; He created rounded mountains that have the appearance of having evolved over millions of years. God, in an instant, created Zion National Park where the water and wind seem to have formed that dramatic valley over centuries.

So when scientists say that the world is 6 billion years old, I don't argue with them. I'm sure that by their standards it does appear that old. God made it so that it was functional and appeared old. But the world, in truth and reality, is quite young. God is Lord over time.

I argued once with a man who said the world had to be old because we see stars explode that are billions of light years away. When we see the light as it reaches earth, we can ascertain when the star exploded and draw the conclusion that the earth is at least that old. But why could God not have made light, which had the appearance of having traveled billions of light years, and why couldn't God have done that in an instant? The Bible says, "And God said, 'Let there be light,' and there was light" (Genesis 1:3). Well, light always takes some time even if it is time of infinitely small amounts. Why can't God create light, which is infinitely old?

This is extremely important, as I will show in the next letter, which will talk about the means God used to create the world.

Letter 70

"The Word, the Word, the Word." That is how Martin Luther responded when asked how God works. He forgives sin by His Word. He creates faith by His Word. He sustains faith by His Word. He heals through His Word. He raised the dead by His Word and He will raise the dead through His Word.

So, it should be no surprise that God created the world simply by speaking His Word. This is the most basic of Christian principles. Everything God does is done by His Word. And as long as it takes God to speak, that is how long it takes God to create things.

In Genesis 1, the story of creation, the expression "and God said" is used nine times as God spoke over the six days. Remarkably, the order in which God created things is roughly the same as the order in which some scientists say that things came into being. The only difference is that God did it quickly and with care and design while scientists say that evolution did it slowly with little care and no design. Some Christians think that maybe God made the world, but He did so slowly so that it appears to have evolved. Why not simply believe that God made evolution happen in six normal days? If He can create slowly, why can't He cause evolution quickly? People ask if the "days" in Genesis 1 are normal. Why not just as easily ask if the billions of years in evolution are normal? Maybe the billions of years happened in six days.

All this is said so that you, Lloyd, will not think less of God simply because He allegedly says things contrary to science. In fact, He says things that are quite scientific. But the main point is that all the power of God is in His Word. Do you want such power? Then listen to His Word.

When I first began these letters, and it's been a year, I was convinced that if you heard the Word by reading it in these letters and could reflect upon it fairly and without pressure, then you would become a Christian.

That's because the same Bible that says God created the heavens and earth by the word of His mouth also says, "[My word] shall not return to Me empty, but it shall accomplish that which I purpose, and shall succeed in the thing for which I sent it" (Isaiah 55:11).

So, Lloyd, when has God spoken to you and created something in you? Many years ago, He said, "Lloyd Bingaman, I baptize you in the name of the Father and of the Son and of the Holy Spirit." And it was so. Baptize means to wash. When He said you were washed—you were washed. In the Gospel God says, "I forgive you your sins." And it is so. Because God says it, you are forgiven. And if you think you are not, well, think again. If God can speak the universe into existence, then He can speak forgiveness upon you. He says "Take, eat, this is My body. Take drink, this is My blood. Given and shed for you for the forgiveness of sins." And it is so. It is His body and blood for your forgiveness. God says it. And it is so.

You can trust the Word of God to be true, and you can trust it also to accomplish what He wants.

◇◇◇◇

Preservation through His Means

Letter 71

God created the world in six days, and He has been taking care of it for thousands of years. And especially He takes care of us.

There is a Bible passage repeated often in the Book of Psalms: "Oh give thanks to the Lord, for He is good, for His steadfast love endures forever" (106:1). Notice that here God gives us two things: goodness and steadfast love (or mercy). You see the same thing in Psalm 23:6 where David says, "Surely goodness and mercy shall follow me all the days of my life, and I shall dwell in the house of the Lord forever."

Goodness is, generally speaking, the things God gives to us in this life. Mercy, generally speaking, is God's faithfulness to His promises to forgive us in Christ and bring us to eternal life.

Think of the things of this life that you have to be thankful for. All are built into creation. God was good when He gave us our bodies that function, in most cases, remarkably well and, in your case, for a very long time. God was good when He provided men of science who figured out how the body works and, subsequently, how to take care of it. God was good to place you into the world at this time when medical science has, to a large degree, been able to extend your life much longer than if you had lived a century ago.

God was good when He gave you parents who not only took care of you when you were tiny and helpless but also taught you to be respectful, thrifty, and responsible—characteristics that have served you very well.

God was good when He gave you a career and a steady job for decades, enabling you to provide for your family and enjoy a modest amount of wealth and some very nice comfort over the years.

God was good not only to give you a wife but also to create you in such a way that you would want one—and vise versa. Through that process God gave you five wonderful daughters. Despite any heartache (for with kids come heartaches), your daughters still richly bless you.

God was good to give us life in America. I suppose we could have been born in Europe during the seventeenth century and died of the plague or buried our children because of it. Or we could have been born in some third world country today and suffer terrible deprivation. What goodness from God we enjoy that we live here and now. Of course, God is good to all people, but relatively, and based on the blessings of this life, we are blessed more than most.

All these blessings are given to us so that this life can have more joy and comfort. They are all from God. They are all means by which He provides us goodness.

Suffering

Letter 72

Even suffering is a form of God's goodness.

Sometimes we suffer because we are stupid. We forget to turn off the oven and our house burns down.

Sometimes we suffer because we do wrong. Someone commits adultery and loses his wife. Someone drinks too much and wrecks his car, his life, or someone else's life.

Sometimes we suffer because others do wrong. Our kids blow our money, and we pay their debts.

But the suffering that is the most difficult is that which we can't explain. Someone we love, God forbid it might even be one of our kids, dies at too young an age. It shouldn't happen, and we can't explain it. A tower falls on someone we love (Luke 13:4). Why did they just happen to be there? Why did it fall then? Like the bridge here in Minneapolis, which collapsed last August, why us? Why then?

In all cases, suffering is a reminder that the wonderful world, which God labels "good," has been corrupted. Even inexplicable suffering is a symptom that something is very wrong. God did not intend for suffering, death, and sorrow. He did not intend for us ever to say, "Why me?" Of course, He did not intend sin.

Suffering always is an indication that this world has been plunged into sin. When Adam and Eve first sinned, their punishment was a changed world. Now those daughters, a great blessing, give their mother pain at birth. Now the earth, source of endless resources, sprouts also thorns and weeds. Now marriage, the holiest of all relationships, is also characterized by friction and power struggles. Now people weep at the graves of loved ones who have turned to dust (Genesis 3:16–19).

Yet, O blessed irony, the suffering that gained entrance into the wonderful creation of God through our guilt is often used by God to lead us to faith, strength, and insight which otherwise would not be ours. And so guilt is relieved.

So I can say that my divorce, the unhappiest period of my life, arguably the most sinful, and clearly that time in which suffering was most acute, has made me value marriage more highly and protect it more fiercely. I have also learned compassion toward those who suffer in difficult marriages—something that, without my divorce, I would not have. And estrangement from my children, painful as it was and temporary, has taught me patience and has helped me be less controlling and more accepting (within reason).

What do we learn from the story of Joseph, who was sold by his brothers into slavery and who spent years in prison and suffered shame and deprivation for half of his life? That saintly man, who was a cocky, insufferable kid, was able to say to his brothers, "You meant evil against me, but God meant it for good" (Genesis 50:20). Suffering taught him to be more patient and forgiving. Bearing his cross taught Joseph to understand that his life is measured not in what he did and not even in what God did through him. Life is measured in what we know about how God works. He accomplishes His greatest work through suffering and the cross.

The Apostles' Creed: Second Article

The Blessing of Jesus

Letter 73

When Martin Luther explained the Second Article of the Apostles' Creed, he concluded with these words, "That I may be His own and live under Him in His kingdom and serve Him in everlasting righteousness, innocence, and blessedness" (*Small Catechism*, Second Article). Blessedness. What does that mean? Everything that Jesus did, from His conception by the Holy Spirit to His death and resurrection to His coming again in glory at the end of time, has this one purpose—That you may be His own and live with Him eternally in blessedness.

God is eternal. He has no beginning and no end. He created us to be eternal just like Him. Although we had a beginning, we will have no end. In Christ, we will spend a blessed eternity with God. What does *bless* or *blessed* mean?

Well, it's the opposite of *curse*. To curse means to speak against someone and to consign him or her to hell. So we curse the devil who came into the garden, brought sin into the world, and has made God's gift of eternity much less than blessed.

Right after Satan corrupted this wonderful world, God cursed him. And in the process, He blessed us, for He promised a Savior who would be a descendant of the woman. He said to the devil, "I will put enmity between you and the woman, and between your offspring and her offspring; He shall bruise your head, and you shall bruise His heal" (Genesis 3:15). This is called the "First Gospel" in the Bible because it is the first promise of a Savior.

Let's analyze this. God is speaking to the devil. He says that the devil along with his minions will constantly be hassling and fighting against the woman and her descendants. But notice that the woman's seed or offspring is called "He." That one seed of the woman will fight the devil. The outcome of that battle will be a blessing to us. The devil will strike some blows against this singular child of the woman. Satan will bruise His heel. But the child of the woman will "crush the head" of Satan. He will triumph.

Let's follow the promise of a child through the Bible. Later in Genesis God promises an "offspring" to Abraham, Isaac, and Jacob, and assures Abraham that through this offspring all the nations of the earth will be blessed (Genesis 12:7; 26:4; 28:14). That is one reason that the Old Testament Jews loved and valued their children. It was through the seed of the woman that one day God would triumph over the devil.

Jacob cheated his brother, Esau, and lied to his father, Isaac, just to get the promise of a seed or offspring. Later, Jacob was careful to bless one of his sons, Judah, with the promise that from his line would come a ruler. "The scepter shall not depart from Judah, nor the ruler's staff from between His feet, until tribute comes to Him; and to Him shall be the obedience of the peoples" (Genesis 49:10). So the promised child will also be a ruler.

David received the same promise: "I will raise up your offspring after you, who shall come from your body. . . . I will establish the throne of His kingdom forever. I will be to Him a Father, and He shall be to Me a Son" (2 Samuel 7:12–14). Isaiah was more specific: "For to us a child is born, to us a son is given . . . and His name shall be called Wonderful Counselor, Mighty God, Everlasting Father, Prince of Peace" (Isaiah 9:6). So this promised child, the seed of the woman, would also be God Himself.

You have a similar promise in the prophecy of Micah: "But you, O Bethlehem Ephrathah, who are too little to be among the clans of Judah, from you shall come forth for Me one who is to be ruler in Israel, whose coming forth is from of old, from ancient days" (5:2). ("Ancient days" means everlasting.) So it appears that this Seed, this child of the woman, will also be the eternal Son of God. All these promises were made hundreds of years before Jesus.

◇◇◇◇

Letter 74

This Seed of the woman was finally born. Paul says, "When the fullness of time had come, God sent forth His Son, born of woman, born under the law, to redeem those who were under the law, so that we might receive adoption as sons" (Galatians 4:4–5). So the Son of God and the son of the woman are the same man—the same little baby.

In Luke, we read about the shepherds in the field, who are told of the little baby born in Bethlehem. From the Old Testament we already know that a seed has been promised who is both the son of a woman and the Son of God. Listen to the birth announcement: "Fear not, for behold, I bring you good news of great joy that will be for all the people. For unto you is born this day in the city of David a Savior, who is Christ the Lord" (Luke 2:10–11). The Lord has come. God is here. He is the promised ruler for He is born in David's city. And He is the Savior. But there is more! "And this will be a sign for you: you will find a baby wrapped in swaddling cloths and lying in a manger" (Luke 2:12). This Lord is the son of the woman. The Lord of all is in a manger. And the baby in the stable rules the world. Luther wrote a hymn with this stanza:

> Ah, Lord, though You created all,
> How weak You are, so poor and small,
> That You should choose to lay Your head
> Where lowly cattle lately fed! (*LSB* 358:9)

This Bible teaching is what theologians call the "two natures of Christ." Christ has two natures. He is God and He is man. He is human and divine. He is the Seed of the woman and the mighty God. Luther put it this way in the Small Catechism: "I believe that Jesus Christ, true God, begotten of the Father from eternity, and also true man, born of the Virgin Mary, is my Lord" (Small Catechism, Second Article).

The promise to Eve that God would send a seed who would crush the head of Satan was fulfilled when the babe of Bethlehem was born. The God-man blesses.

Whatever this baby does, God does. And what Jesus intended to do as He grew up, God had planned. The contest between Jesus and the devil has begun. Your life with God for eternity is at stake. God wants to bless you in Jesus. And the devil does not want that.

An initial skirmish takes place in Matthew 2. It starts out innocently enough. Wise men come to worship baby Jesus. He must be God or they would not worship Him. But the devil can't have that. So he hatches a plot to end the cosmic conflict before it has even begun. Wickedly, soldiers are dispatched who "killed all the male children in Bethlehem and in all that region who were two years old or under" (Matthew 2:16). But the battle of the ages will not end so abruptly. God warns Joseph in a dream to protect the little baby.

Later, the people from Jesus' hometown try to kill Him prematurely (Luke 4:29). But, again, the devil is thwarted. Jesus walks away from the murderous crowd. The devil must confront the God-man in face-to-face combat. And the devil knows the predicted outcome. He will bruise the child's heel; the Christ will crush his head. The battle began in the wilderness, continued through various episodes in Jesus' life, reached its climax in a garden, and is consummated on the cross.

Letter 75

Knowing that Jesus was going to defeat him on the cross, the devil tried desperately to keep Jesus from going to that cross. He tried to get Him killed, as mentioned last time. The temptation in the wilderness was more formidable; it was an attempt to dissuade Jesus from His plan to die.

You can read about God's plan in Philippians 2:5–11. God wants Jesus to be humbled, to become nothing, to be a servant and to become obedient until He died on a cross. That's the plan (which we'll call Plan A). God knows that there are wonderful blessings to be gained for you and me through the death of Christ.

God's plan is completed as follows: after Christ dies a shameful death, God will exalt Him, raise Him from the dead, and give Him a lofty name. Everyone will bow to Christ when He comes in glory and everyone will then know that He is Lord. So the plan is humiliation and shame followed by glory and blessing.

But the devil had Plan B, which you can read about in Matthew 4 and Luke 4. The devil takes Jesus to a mountaintop, shows Him all the kingdoms of the world, and promises that all this will belong to Jesus if He will only worship him. So the devil's plan is that Jesus could avoid the humiliation and shame of Plan A and go straight to the glory. What the devil conveniently does not say is that in Plan A, you and I are forgiven of our sins and accepted by God—we are blessed. In plan B, we simply go to hell.

So here are the two plans. Plan A: Jesus suffers hell on the cross and we are forgiven and blessed. Plan B: Jesus does not suffer, but we end up going to hell. The devil knows that Jesus will crush him on the cross. So he desperately wants Jesus to avoid the cross. Ultimately, Jesus tells the devil to get away, and that rather formidable battle goes to Jesus. But a bit later Jesus tells His disciples that He must go to Jerusalem, suffer many things, and finally be killed. Peter rebukes Him: "Far be it from You, Lord! This shall never happen to You" (Matthew 16:22). Peter just didn't get it. He didn't understand that Jesus had come into the world to crush the devil, and this crushing would only occur through His death. Only Jesus' death could forgive sins. Only Jesus' death could undo the sin and corruption that Satan had inflicted upon our first parents in the garden. The devil was behind Peter's comments. It was Satan trying again to dissuade Jesus from the cross. That's why Jesus gave such a stern and pointed answer to His friend: "Get behind Me, Satan" (Matthew 16:23)! Anyone who tries to keep Jesus from the cross is of the devil. And, Lloyd, anyone who tries to distract you from the cross is of the devil.

It happened throughout His life that Jesus was encouraged to grab glory for Himself before He suffered. People wanted to make Him king. People wanted Him to settle earthly matters rather than settle eternal heavenly matters. But Plan A had to do with heaven, eternity, and blessings from God. The most dramatic battle was in a garden—not the Garden of Eden but the Garden of Gethsemane.

Jesus in the Garden

Letter 76

Jesus tells His disciples His last will and testament. He speaks of His body given for them and His blood shed for the sins of many. He intends to die. How strange this must sound to those twelve whose sole intent, it seems, is to prevent Jesus from giving His body and shedding His blood. He then leads His disciples to the Garden of Gethsemane where He engages the devil in a major battle. It's the Seed of the woman against the serpent.

He says to His disciples, "My soul is very sorrowful, even to death" (Matthew 26:38). Then He prays a prayer to which He knows the answer. "My Father, if it be possible, let this cup pass from Me; nevertheless, not as I will, but as You will" (Matthew 26:39).

This little prayer is powerful. Jesus knows that He must be crucified. He knows that He will suffer physical pain. He knows that His pain and death will effectively crush the head of Satan, for through His death He will earn forgiveness for all people. He knows that Satan is at that very moment trying to make Him so afraid that He would back away from this shameful death. And Jesus does not want to die. Who would? Then things get worse. He wants His disciples to stay awake, but He returns to find them sleeping!

He is all alone praying to His father, who is serving Him up to death. Here is what is happening. Remember, Lloyd, I mentioned a few letters ago Plan A and Plan B. Remember Plan A, which is God's plan. Isaiah had predicted, "He was pierced for our transgressions; He was crushed for our iniquities. . . . It was the will of the Lord to crush Him; He has put Him to grief" (Isaiah 53:5, 10). Plan A required Jesus to suffer so that the disciples could avoid hell. But why should Jesus even care for false friends who can't even stay awake and who would, momentarily, run away from Him? Should God crush Him for them? Why would He do that? And why would He suffer for you? Think of the times you have slept when you should have prayed or been indifferent to the things of God. Think of the times you have questioned God's love. Why then, should Jesus suffer for you?

Or maybe Jesus should follow Plan B. That is the devil's plan. Avoid the cross. Let each man fend for himself. Let the disciples face God themselves. Jesus could snap His fingers and make all of His enemies fall. He could call upon heaven and God would send ten thousand angels to defend Him from this impending death (Mathew 26:53–54). True, Plan B means that you and I will end up crushed by Satan. But we have it coming, right? Our indifference to such a predicament, you would think, would be a serious motivator for Jesus to choose Plan B. Why should Jesus go through the crushing pain and abandonment of the cross when He does not have to? I would not do it. My instinct for self-preservation is too strong.

No wonder Jesus sweats great drops of blood. You would, too, if you were confronted with that choice. No wonder the angels came to minister to Him. He certainly couldn't rely on friends.

Satan is gleeful. Jesus, he thinks, is wavering and weak. Satan almost has Him. He's going to walk away, thinks the devil. Then come those stark and saving works of a Son's sacrificial obedience, "Not as I will, but as You will." Jesus knew God's will: "It was the will of the LORD to crush Him."

Satan watches in horror as Jesus resolutely goes to the cross. Every temptation that he had successfully worked upon you; every moral defeat for which you are accountable; every time your instincts for self-preservation selfishly lead you to ignore the needs of others or the will of God; every guilty pleasure; every occasional lapse; every intentional and unintentional transgression; every single time the devil won the day with you—every sin is forgiven. Satan is undone. Good Friday was a very bad day for the devil.

The Seed of the woman has crushed the head of the serpent. He who in a garden once overcame has likewise by a garden been overcome.

◇◇◇◇

Letter 77

On the cross Jesus patiently bears the sin of humanity. And from the cross He cries to God, "Father, forgive them, for they know not what they do" (Luke 23:34). You recall that four letters ago I promised to define the word *bless.* To bless means "to speak a good word." It's similar to the word *benediction.* At the end of every Divine Service, the pastor speaks the Benediction when he says, "The Lord bless you and keep you." Benediction means, "To speak a good word upon someone." Take it apart: From *diction* we have "dictate" or "speak something." From *bene* we have "beneficial." So *benediction* is "to dictate good."

From the cross you hear a benediction, a blessing, and an absolution all in one phrase: "Father, forgive them." Jesus is asking His Father to take away our sins. He bases this request not on the fact that God is a nice guy, or on the belief that we are fundamentally good or that we have really tried or even that we are ignorant. "They don't know what they do," is not an excuse. It's an indictment. He's not asking God to forgive because we don't know any better. God forgives us because Jesus died for us. Our ignorance is not an excuse. It reflects further need of forgiveness. We are not only cruel and perverse by killing Jesus; we are arrogant and don't even know who it is we are crucifying. I don't know which is worse.

The only reason that Jesus can presume to ask His Father to forgive us is that Jesus is, at that very moment, carrying our sins in His body. God is asked to undo the curse of Satan because Jesus has just crushed the old evil foe. The Father's answer to His Son is, well, a miracle.

Does God forgive the sins of His people simply because Jesus asks? The answer is "Yes." And He shows us that His answer is "Yes" by raising Jesus from the dead.

The resurrection is God's way of saying publicly that He has accepted the sacrifice of Jesus. It's like God is saying, "Jesus asked Me to forgive you all of your sins. He asked this not just for those who were actually beneath the cross. He asked this on behalf of all people who had ever lived and ever would live." God continues, "How can I answer this request of Jesus so that everyone will know? How do I honor His request? I know what I will do. I will raise Him from the dead. That will prove to everyone that whatever Jesus asks on behalf of the people I will do." Paul writes that Jesus "was delivered up [to death] for our trespasses and raised for our justification" (Romans 4:25). All the sins of the world were placed on the crucified Jesus. "He was crushed for our iniquities" (Isaiah 53:5). And all the forgiveness in the world moved God to raise Him from the grave. That's why Paul can write elsewhere that "if Christ has not been raised, your faith is futile and you are still in your sins" (1 Corinthians 15:17). Paul knew that Christ had been raised. He saw the resurrected Christ. Five hundred people also were witnesses of that event.

So, for the last two thousand years people have gone all over the world announcing to people everywhere that Jesus was raised from the dead. This announcement is an absolution. It is publicizing to all that our sins have been forgiven and that Jesus has crushed the devil.

In fact, if you think about it, the resurrection of Jesus from the dead was the world's loudest blessing. It was God saying for all time and for all people, "I forgive you." It is the final and eternally valid absolution of all sins. It is the basis for all subsequent absolutions. It is God's benediction on the Divine Service, which Jesus performed once for all on the cross and continues to perform every Sunday morning. It is God's way of saying, "You may be His own and live with Him in His kingdom with blessedness."

◇◇◇◇

The Apostles' Creed: Third Article

Crushing Satan Today

Letter 78

In the last chapter of his Letter to the Romans, Paul says a very strange thing: "The God of peace will soon crush Satan under your feet. The grace of our Lord Jesus Christ be with you" (Romans 16:20). What makes this unusual is that it takes the idea of crushing Satan, which we know was accomplished by Christ on the cross, and it talks about it in the future as if it has yet to be accomplished. How can this be?

We can think of crushing Satan the same way Luther explains the forgiveness of sins. Here's what Luther says:

> We treat of the forgiveness of sins in two ways. First, how it is achieved and won. Second, how it is distributed and given to us. Christ has achieved it on the cross. . . . He has distributed and given it through the Word, as also in the gospel, where it is preached. (AE 40:213–14)

Just as we can talk about forgiveness in two ways we can also talk about the crushing of Satan in two ways. Satan was crushed once and for all on the cross. Yet, Satan is also crushed each time the Word of Christ is spoken. Satan is crushed whenever a little baby is baptized. Satan is crushed each time you go to the Lord's Supper. Satan is crushed whenever your pastor absolves your sins.

Historically, Jesus crushed Satan. Satan is crushed each time Jesus is applied to your life.

This introduces the Third Article of the Creed: "I believe in the Holy Spirit." Basically the job of the Holy Spirit is to take the work that Christ did and give it to us today. Jesus forgave sins once for all. The Holy Spirit applies that forgiveness to you today through the Word and Sacraments. Jesus lived and died to earn salvation. The Holy Spirit bestows that salvation to us through the Word and Sacraments. Jesus lived and died to redeem us. Each time the Holy Spirit speaks the Word of Christ to us, we are redeemed from sin. Jesus crushed the head of the serpent through His agony and bloody sweat. Each time you hear the story of the cross, Satan is crushed. That is why we can say that Satan has been crushed and we can repeat with Paul, "The God of peace will soon crush Satan under your feet."

What makes the power of the Holy Spirit so precious is that little, old, helpless people like you and me can tap into it any time we need. We actually have power over the devil right this moment. Whenever we speak the Word, read the Bible, reflect upon Christ's work for us—or as you read these letters—God is using this Word to crush Satan under your feet. In a sense, we can crush Satan simply by speaking or hearing the claims of Jesus.

> Though devils all the world should fill,
> All eager to devour us,
> We tremble not, we fear no ill;
> They shall not overpow'r us.
> This world's prince may still
> Scowl fierce as he will,
> He can harm us none.
> He's judged; the deed is done;
> One little word can fell him. (*LSB* 656:3)

This is from Luther's hymn "A Mighty Fortress Is Our God." Notice that Luther says here again that Satan has already been judged. That happened on the cross. Yet one little word can fell him. That is the Word of Christ that we hear every day. When that Word is spoken and heard, the Holy Spirit is working, and Satan is crushed.

◇◇◇◇

The Holy Spirit

A Holy Conversation

Letter 79

Before I delve too deeply into the Holy Spirit—who He is and what He does—it is necessary again to talk about our needs as human beings.

I can tell you a hundred times about all the wonderful things that Jesus has done for you and I could anticipate a single consistent response: "But if Jesus has done all these things, then why do I still feel so far from Him? Why do I find it so hard to believe? If the devil has been crushed—and who would not want to believe this—then why is he having his way with me so easily and so consistently?" Here is the answer.

Your entire life has been one long conversation with God about how you stand before Him.

You spoke first. Even before you were aware of much, you were selfish. It was inevitable that you would strive to please yourself. I know this because it's Paul's description of all of us who "lived in the passions of our flesh, carrying out the desires of the body and the mind" (Ephesians 2:3). I am convinced that most of us would realize this natural selfishness even if we did not read it in the Bible. "I want that," is everyone's first thought. Whether it's food or a change of diapers or a little cuddling or a nap—our first thoughts are for ourselves. That is why parents have to teach their children to think of others. We rarely have to teach our kids to think of themselves first or to do the things they want. It's a recent and unnecessary mantra of our day to encourage people to look out for number one. We all look out for ourselves by nature. So our first words and thoughts were not of God and not of others. They were of self.

Then the Holy Spirit, who is God, spoke. Into this selfish life He came with Baptism. For some it was early in their lives; for others it happened when they could actually reflect upon it. For some it never happened—what a tragedy. In Baptism the Holy Spirit forgives your selfishness. More than that, He also kills that selfishness and redirects your thoughts. Now, He points your heart and mind to higher things, to things above, to Jesus who has redeemed us from our own selfishness. "I baptize you with water for repentance," says God (Matthew 3:11). He's talking to you to change you.

But you talked back. First, you said something selfish. "I like my old ways better. I like stealing rather than helping. I like cheating—whether on a test, or in marriage, or in life—more than I like being fair or keeping my word. I like the heady feeling of defiance more than the tranquil feeling of submission, either to God or to human authority. I actually prefer sin."

Then, having elevated your desires above His, you said something even more selfish. "I can't trust You, God. You claimed that You would forgive me, but I don't see forgiveness. You said You would live in me, but I don't feel Your presence." (Never mind that we would prefer not to feel His presence—at least on His terms.) "I can't trust You, God. You said that You would take care of me, and here I am having to take care of myself." (Never mind that we would much prefer taking care of ourselves than actually trusting God to do so.)

So God speaks again. "These thoughts and inclinations of yours are wrong. I suppose I could destroy you, but I much prefer to save you."

The Continuing Conversation

Letter 80

Into your sinful and selfish condition God speaks again: "I forgive you still. But you will constantly turn away from Me unless I do something dramatic—no, not dramatic—I will do something plain and simple. It must be small. It must be smaller than small. It must be reprehensible, even loathsome." God, who had sent His Son to be a small and loathsome Savior while dying on the tree, now speaks to us in a small and loathsome way. "Unless you eat the flesh of the Son of Man and drink His blood, you have no life in you" (John 6:53).

Some Bible scholars take these words to be a reference to the Lord's Supper. Others believe they are a reference to receiving the Word with faith. Either way, they are not appealing to our personal sense of self-worth and value.

Here is what the Lord is saying: "I am so tired of you. All you do is think of yourself. You believe in Me only when My judgments agree with yours. You trust Me only when My plans agree with yours. You only love Me when I tell you things you agree with. You repent only when it is convenient and painless. You serve Me only after you have served yourself, and you are never finished serving yourself. Now, do you want Me? Then eat My flesh and drink My blood. You must stop being yourself. You must discontinue every sense of self-preservation. You must never justify your behavior again. You must die to yourself. You must cease to exist as Lloyd Bingaman, citizen of earth. You can only exist as Lloyd Bingaman, citizen of heaven. And leave everything to Me. My kingdom comes through death and sacrifice. It comes only through the sacrificial flesh of Jesus and His holy, precious blood, which dripped from His wounds. It will be yours only when you cease to live. It will be yours when My flesh and blood are more precious to you than your own."

You answer back, "How do I do this?"

He responds. "You do this by killing all of your own judgments, opinions, feelings, plans, hopes, loves, interests, and anything else that might be important to you. In their place you have nothing but Jesus—His flesh scourged and beaten and His blood poured out from His wounds. Anything that means more to you than My flesh and blood will kill you."

You reply, "I don't think I am capable of that level of commitment and sacrifice."

He answers, "Of course you aren't. That's why I sent My Son. What do you think procured this flesh and blood that saves you? It was His commitment for you. Quit thinking about commitment and start thinking about death. You must die. (Of course, Lloyd, we all pray that in this life you continue to live. I speak of dying in regard to your own opinions and values, not dying in your own body.) You must die in order to live."

But we argue with the Holy Spirit. "No one wants to die. How can God encourage or even cause death? Didn't Jesus come so that I could live?"

He answers, "The Lord kills and brings to life; He brings down to Sheol and raises up" (1 Samuel 2:6). God kills when He makes us give up on ourselves. God raises up when He shows us Jesus.

The Conversation of Worship

Letter 81

Lloyd, Jan tells me that you have joined the church to which you belonged many years ago. She also says that you have taken some instruction at the church in order to reaffirm your faith. I trust that you are excited about this. I am! The Holy Spirit works through the Word and the Sacrament, and typically you receive these every time you attend the worship service. In fact, when you think about it, the Sunday service is really a continuation of the conversation between you and God that I have been talking about in the last couple of letters.

The primary speaker in the church service is God. That's why Lutherans call the Sunday service the Divine Service. It is because in this service God serves us with His Word and Sacrament. But we do some conversing as well. We respond to God.

For example, the service typically begins with us confessing our sins, and God responds through the pastor with the word of forgiveness. Then we respond back to God by singing a psalm or a hymn.

In the course of the Divine Service, the Holy Spirit tells us of the many things Jesus did for us. And He does so through the songs that are sung every week. First, we sing what's called the "Kyrie"—"Lord, have mercy upon us." That reminds us that God heard the prayers of His people long ago as they waited for the Savior to come. It is an Advent theme.

Then we sing what is called the "Gloria in Excelsis." Through that song the Holy Spirit reminds us of Christmas, for we sing, "Glory to God in the highest and on earth peace, good will to man."

Later in the service we say the Creed, which is a reminder of the many things Jesus has done for us. It is the emphasis of Epiphany, which is the season after Christmas when we think of Jesus showing Himself to us. Epiphany means "to shine upon."

Then we sing a song called the "Sanctus." This is just before Holy Communion. In that song we sing, "Holy, Holy, Holy." *Sanctus* is the Latin word meaning "holy." Then we sing "Hosanna in the highest," which is what the people sang as Jesus entered Jerusalem on a donkey. So it's a celebration of Palm Sunday. *Hosanna* is the Hebrew word for "He saves." When we sing the Sanctus, we are saying that the Holy One saves us.

Immediately after the Sanctus, the pastor speaks the words of Christ's Last Supper. It's an observance of Maundy Thursday, which some call Holy Thursday. Shortly after that we sing, "O Christ, Thou Lamb of God, that takest away the sin of the world." That song, called the "Agnus Dei" is sung as an observance of Good Friday when Jesus gave up His life for us.

Finally, after Communion, we sing what's called the "Nunc Dimittis." That is a celebration of Easter as we talk about our own resurrection when we sing, "Lord, now lettest Thou Thy servant depart in peace according to Thy word, for mine eyes have seen Thy salvation." It's like taking Communion has prepared us to go to heaven.

So, Lloyd, you have at least six or seven Christian seasons or holidays every Sunday: Advent, Christmas, Epiphany, Palm Sunday, Maundy Thursday, Good Friday, and Easter.

Through the Divine Service, the church sings songs that allow a celebration of the entire Christian message. What a great conversation that is! You are speaking, and through the service God is speaking and blessing.

◇◇◇◇

Letter 82

All this about conversations and worship may seem to make the Holy Spirit a bit complicated. So let me make Him simple.

The Holy Spirit is the press secretary for Jesus. He does not say things that bring attention to Himself; He says things that glorify Jesus, teach us about Jesus, or witness to Jesus. That's what Jesus says in the Gospel of John: "The Helper, the Holy Spirit, whom the Father will send in My name, He will teach you all things and bring to your remembrance all that I have said to you. . . .When the Helper comes, whom I will send to you from the Father, the Spirit of truth, who proceeds from the Father, He will bear witness about Me. . . .When the Spirit of truth comes, . . . He will glorify Me" (John 14:26; 15:26; 16:13–14).

Everything the Holy Spirit does makes you trust and love Jesus more. So Paul says, "No one can say, 'Jesus is Lord' except in the Holy Spirit'" (1 Corinthians 12:3).

Do guilt trips and commands make you love and trust Jesus? Do they forgive your sins? No. Then the Holy Spirit does not use them. He may convict us through them, but He does not use them to glorify Jesus. Do incessant church requests and demands for more money make you love Jesus and trust Him? No. Then they are not what the Holy Spirit uses. Do the harpings of some religious leaders that you have to make a stronger commitment make you trust and love Jesus? No. Then that is not the Holy Spirit working.

Does your Baptism in which God washed away your sins in Christ and created faith in your heart make you trust Jesus? It should, and surely it does. So the Holy Spirit is working in Baptism. When you hear the Gospel that God has sent His Son to take upon Himself your sins and weaknesses, that Jesus has died for you and that in Him you have eternal life—does that make you trust and love Jesus? Then the Holy Spirit is at work in the Gospel. When you go to the Supper to eat Christ's body and drink His blood for the forgiveness of sins, does that make you trust Jesus? Then the Holy Spirit is working.

Anything that forgives you your sins in Christ is used by the Spirit. Anything that does not, is not.

The reason church services are so important is not that you are doing something religious. The church service is not a way for you to show your commitment. Rather, in the Divine Service the Holy Spirit speaks to you of Jesus, baptizes you into Christ, and gives you the body and blood of our Lord. Through these blessings He forgives you and leads you to trust and love Jesus more.

I hope, Lloyd, that your health will hold up so that you can attend church services for a long time—not because it is such a good thing to do, but because God, the Holy Spirit, gives you so much through His Gospel and Sacraments.

As Christmas approached in 2007, Jan expressed a desire to go to Fresno again and, convinced that this would be Lloyd's last Christmas, she arranged to spend the holiday with her father. Her report to me was grim as Lloyd appeared to be as gaunt and weak as he had been 18 months earlier when the letters began. So I wrote the letters with a more eschatological tone.

The Work of Jesus

Letter 83

Lloyd, I'd like to share with you what the Bible says about heaven and eternal life. When Jesus died on the cross for you, He said, "It is finished" (John 19:30). Some time ago I wrote a number of letters to you concerning what "It" refers to in the sentence of John 19:30. When Jesus said, "It is finished," He had finished suffering. He had finished carrying away your sins. He had finished bearing the accusations of the Law so that you wouldn't have to. He was finished redeeming you. "It" has one more referent. It means that He has also finished opening the gates of heaven for you. In John 14:2, Jesus says that He is going to prepare a place for you. His going refers to His innocent life and His sacrificial death. He went to the cross to prepare a place. When He said, "It is finished," He was referring to His construction of a heavenly home for you. He had finished furnishing heaven for you, Lloyd.

I'm sure, Lloyd, that you've heard a hundred jokes about lawyers, pastors, priests, rabbis, undertakers, actors, and degenerates who have all died and gone to heaven, only to meet Peter at the "pearly gates" and have a conversation with him. These conversations usually refer to some condition that must be fulfilled by someone in order for them to get into heaven. The truth of the matter is, Lloyd, that Jesus has already met all the conditions for your entrance into heaven. When He died for you, He had finished preparing a place.

Christ died to save us from sin and all its consequences. Before there was sin in the world there was no death, no pain, no sorrow over loss, no discomfort, and no worries. So, through Christ, not only are you forgiven by the death of Jesus, you also are promised that pain, sorrow, worry, doubt, suffering, deprivation, and even death itself, will, someday, no longer be part of our experience.

It says in Revelation 7:14 that Christians have "washed their robes and made them white in the blood of the Lamb." (That means we have been forgiven by the death of Jesus and through His Word and Sacraments.) Of those who have washed their robes it says: "They shall hunger no more, neither thirst anymore; the sun shall not strike them, nor any scorching heat. For the Lamb in the midst of the throne will be their shepherd, and He will guide them to springs of living water, and God will wipe away every tear from their eyes" (Revelation 7:16–17).

"Behold, the dwelling place of God is with man. He will dwell with them, and they will be His people, and God Himself will be with them as their God. He will wipe away every tear from their eyes, and death shall be no more, neither shall there be mourning, nor crying, nor pain anymore, for the former things have passed away" (Revelation 21:3–4).

There is a very comforting hymn that I sing whenever I get a bit tired of this life:

> When from the dust of death I rise
> To claim my mansion in the skies,
> This then shall be my only plea:
> Jesus hath lived and died for me. (*LSB* 563:5)

Heaven is that place where you will have only joy. It's a place where there will be no more difficulties. It is made available to us through Jesus, who lived and died for us.

Heaven

The Grace of Jesus

Letter 84

How do we get to heaven? Is there something we can do to earn our place? No. The only way to heaven is through Jesus. His death prepared it for us, and He is the One who took all obstacles away.

And the way to have Jesus, Lloyd, is something which I trust you have come to know through these letters as well as through the ministry of your church. Jesus can be and is yours through His Word and Sacrament.

Jan, who is traveling to see you even as I write, has informed me that your pastor came on Christmas to give you the Sacrament of Christ's body and blood. This wonderful meal has been called "a medicine of immortality" by some of the Church Fathers because it gives us Jesus' true body and blood and with that the forgiveness of sins. So the Lord's Supper brings you Jesus, who gets you to heaven.

Baptism also gets you to heaven. Paul says that we were crucified with Christ in Baptism. Further, "We were buried therefore with Him by baptism into death, in order that, just as Christ was raised from the dead by the glory of the Father, we too might walk in newness of life" (Romans 6:4). He goes on to promise that "if we have been united with Him in a death like His, we shall certainly be united with Him in a resurrection like His" (v. 5). In Baptism we died. Our old self is dead. It is Christ who now lives for us and in us through Baptism. We have died and been raised in Him.

The Word of the Gospel, the Good News of Jesus, gets you to heaven. That Word never perishes. "The Word of our God will stand forever" (Isaiah 40:8). And those to whom God speaks His promises have the privilege of hearing and living forever by that Word. So John also calls the Word of God "an eternal Gospel" (Revelation 14:6). And this Word saves us eternally.

In the Gospel of John, Jesus promises that those who know His Word and trust in Him through that Word will never die. "If anyone keeps My word, he will never see death" (John 8:51). In this passage the word *keeps* does not mean "obey" or "comply with." Rather, it means "guards" or "retains," like you keep your money in a bank. Jesus also says, "My sheep hear My voice, and I know them, and they follow Me. I give them eternal life, and they will never perish, and no one will snatch them out of My hand" (John 10:27–28). "I am the resurrection and the life. Whoever believes in Me, though he die, yet shall he live, and everyone who lives and believes in Me shall never die" (John 11:25–26).

So you get to heaven by the Word, Baptism, and the Lord's Supper. These three are the containers that bring to you the grace of Jesus. They give Jesus to you, and they connect you to Him.

There is another hymn that I tend to sing whenever I need a reminder of how Jesus is given to me and how I can have Him:

> Here stands the font before our eyes,
> Telling how God has received us.
> The altar recalls Christ's sacrifice
> And what His Supper here gives us.
> Here sound the Scriptures that proclaim
> Christ yesterday, today the same,
> And evermore, our Redeemer. (*LSB* 645:4)

Jesus is the same yesterday, today, and forever. His Word and Sacraments give Him to us. He makes us ready for heaven. Because of Jesus—His life and death for you—and because of His Word and Sacraments, Lloyd, you are ready for heaven. And in heaven you will see Jesus.

◇◇◇◇

You've Always Been Closer Than You Think

 Letter 85

Our sadness when we face death should never be over the one whose death is close at hand. Rather, our sadness is for ourselves because we will miss you. It is a type of selfishness in a good way. We don't want to be without you. You are truly blessed to be so close to eternity.

I once asked a first-and-second-grade Sunday School class this question: "How do you get to heaven?" A little boy shot his hand up and waved it in the air as a sign to me that he had the definitive answer. I expected him to say, "Jesus takes you there." After all, we do sing in the Christmas song "Bless all the dear children in Thy tender care, And take us to heaven to live with Thee there" (*LSB* 365:3). I certainly thought he would say something about faith in Jesus. "Well," he said, "first you have to die." All the teachers laughed because it was not what we expected. But it is true. You can't get to heaven unless you die.

Or, is it true?

Yes, in the Bible heaven is that place where we go to be with Jesus when we die and when He comes to get us. But in a very real sense we have heaven and eternal life on earth right now if we have Jesus. Jesus said, "I am the resurrection and the life . . . everyone who lives and believes in Me shall never die" (John 11:25–26). So through Jesus we escape death. And in John 6, Jesus says, "Whoever feeds on My flesh and drinks My blood has eternal life" (v. 54). Notice that it says that you *have* eternal life (present tense). It does not merely say that you *will* have eternal life. And in John 10, Jesus says, "My sheep hear My voice. . . . I give them eternal life, and they will never perish, and no one will snatch them out of My hand" (vv. 27–28). Notice it does not say merely that Jesus *will* give us eternal life. He gives us (present tense) eternal life.

We have eternal life right now. But if that is the case, then what is death? Death is being brought from one stage of life to the next. Now we know Jesus through His Word and Sacraments by faith. In heaven we will know Him face-to-face. But we always know Him—both now and then. "Now we see in a mirror dimly, but then face to face. Now I know in part; then I shall know fully, even as I have been fully known" (1 Corinthians 13:12).

There is another hymn that we sang around the dinner table growing up which goes like this:

> Thou hast died for my transgression,
> All my sins on Thee were laid;
> Thou hast won for me salvation,
> On the cross my debt was paid.
> From the grave I shall arise
> And shall meet Thee in the skies.
> Death itself is transitory;
> I shall lift my head in glory. (*LSB* 548:2)

Death is transitory. That means it is like a transit that brings you from one place to another. It rapidly transports you from knowing Jesus here to seeing Jesus there. You could, I suppose, call death "HART": Heavenly Area Rapid Transit.

So everyone who knows Jesus enjoys eternal life right at this moment and death merely brings us to that place where, best of all, you will see Jesus.

◇◇◇◇

HEAVEN

Positively

Letter 86

The Bible tells us what we will *not* have in heaven—pain, sorrow, work, and tribulation. I suppose, Lloyd, that you did not get to church this Christmas since you were in the hospital. So you may not have heard God's people sing "Joy to the World." The third stanza goes like this:

> No more let sins and sorrows grow
> Nor thorns infest the ground;
> He comes to make His blessings flow
> Far as the curse is found. (*LSB* 387:3)

I think that you should have the girls sing it right now as they read this. A little yuletide cheer is always nice.

The hymnwriter Isaac Watts shows that he understands heaven. Sin had caused curses to come upon us—death, pain, sorrow, work, and thorns infesting the ground and making work difficult. In Christ, these are all gone.

What is heaven like? There will be good food there. In Revelation 22, heaven is described as a place with a river of crystal-clear water flowing from the throne of the Lamb. On either side there is a tree that yields fruit every month. These are called the "trees of life." So in heaven you will never get hungry. It's not like food will be obsolete, God forbid. Rather, we will always have it. And the food will be sumptuous. Isaiah describes heaven as a mountain where "the LORD of hosts will make for all peoples a feast of rich food, a feast of well-aged wine, of rich food, of rich food full of marrow, of aged wine well refined" (Isaiah 25:6).

Heaven is also described as a place of singing. In the Book of Revelation, which tells of heaven, there are a dozen songs that the saints will sing in heaven. One song is similar to our Sanctus, which we sing before taking Holy Communion. "This is the Feast" is based on Revelation 5:12–13, 19:5–9. In our church we sing this song every Sunday for seven weeks after Easter. Other churches sing it even more often. We need to practice the songs we will be singing in heaven.

Heaven is compared to a wedding feast (Matthew 22:1–14). If you like weddings with food, drink, singing, and enjoying the best this life has to offer, then you will enjoy heaven.

Heaven also is a place of light. With the invention of the light bulb we take light for granted. But imagine life before electricity. One night as Paul was preaching, a man fell asleep, fell out of a window, and died. That's because they had only oil lamps, which would eat up the oxygen in the air and make you fall asleep. And I know that up at the lake, where there is no electricity, we always had to strain to read or play cards after the sun went down. Jesus is the Light of the World. He permeates heaven. In heaven, "night will be no more. They will need no light of lamp or sun, for the Lord God will be their light" (Revelation 22:5).

So heaven is a bright and cheery place where all your needs are met. There will be people you love with great food and wine, lots of good music and singing, and plenty of light. And, best of all, you will see Jesus.

Jan informed me that Lloyd was often so medicated that he had a hard time staying awake while the letters were read to him. All of his daughters were there and listened along with him. It occurred to me that whatever I wrote at this point would probably be "read, marked, learned, and taken to heart" more by them than their father. So the next couple of letters were for them.

◇◇◇◇

Getting to Heaven

The Tribulation

Letter 87

You get to heaven through Jesus Christ. Heaven is a place that He prepared for you through His death. You are prepared for heaven through the Gospel and Sacraments. Heaven is truly a wonderful feast with food and wine and millions of people, all who know the voice of their Savior.

The Bible tells us what God has planned for His children. First, the Lord will take us from this "veil of tears." True, for me, life has provided more joy than sorrow, but life is a struggle often enough. The Bible calls it a "tribulation." Tribulation is not a specific seven-year time period that some people foolishly hold to. It is a description of your life and mine. Life is a tribulation because it is often painful to live in a sinful world. It is tedious to work all your life. And at the end of it sometimes all you can say is, "Vanity of vanities! All is vanity. What does man gain by all the toil at which he toils under the sun?" (Ecclesiastes 1:2–3). It is often profoundly difficult to live like a Christian.

The tribulation of life will continue either until Jesus returns in glory or until you die. When you die, you go to be with Jesus, which is the second event God promises. At the precise moment of death, according to the Bible, "the dust returns to the earth as it was, and the spirit returns to God who gave it" (Ecclesiastes 12:7). From our perspective, death is a tragedy, and the Bible often talks of it that way. It is tragic because God did not intend death when He created the world. That's why He sent Jesus. From God's perspective, death is simply another step in the gracious plan He has for you.

At the moment of death you will be with Jesus. Your body will be in the grave. And years will go by—perhaps a couple, perhaps a couple thousand. At some point in time, which only God knows and which we should not waste our time trying to predict, Jesus will return. But I'm getting ahead of myself.

God has provided certain signs or occurrences along the way that serve as reminders that something far better is in store for His people. In society there are wars and rumors of war, animosity, and wickedness. In the world there are famines, earthquakes, and other disasters. In the Church there are false Christs, false teachers, and persecutions of Christians, but the Gospel is spread despite all this (Matthew 24:14).

Luther was completely convinced that all the signs of his day portended an immediate return of Jesus. Many at the time of the apostles felt the same. Second Thessalonians was written to correct the false but pious notion that Jesus would return before any Christians died. Throughout the ages, there have been many periods when expectations of Christ's second coming ran high. I'm sure you remember at the turn of the millennium the misguided expectations of many who predicted direly that the world was coming to an end. But Jesus has yet to return. So we wait. While we wait, people who know Jesus continue to die and go to be with their Lord.

But the day is certainly coming. I do not know when. God tells us to be prepared at all times and watch fervently for that day. And on that day, as the Scriptures tell us, all nations "will see the Son of Man coming on the clouds of heaven with power and great glory. And He will send out His angels with a loud trumpet call, and they will gather His elect from the four winds, from one end of heaven to the other" (Matthew 24:30–31).

◇◇◇◇

The Resurrection

Letter 88

On the eventful and dramatic day you ascend to heaven, three wonderful things will happen. First, you will be raised from the dead. You will get your body back, but it will not be the body that has become weak and riddled with cancer. "So is it with the resurrection of the dead. What is sown is perishable; what is raised is imperishable. It is sown in dishonor; it is raised in glory. It is sown in weakness; it is raised in power. It is sown a natural body; it is raised a spiritual body" (1 Corinthians 15:42–44). That's pretty nice.

The Bible speaks about the resurrection often. It is emphasized about fifty times as often as the Bible talks about the moment of death. That's because the moment you die is not the end of the story. But the day of resurrection, when all flesh will see Jesus—that is the consummate moment of all times. It is truly something to anticipate eagerly. Let me give you a couple of examples of anticipation from the Bible.

Job was a man known for his patience. He was constantly being hassled by his wife and friends with bad counsel. They wanted him either to curse God or to question Him. Job needed patience. God tested him by taking away his wealth and children. Job did not want to question God. He did not want to think that he somehow deserved his misfortune. Job was particularly agitated when his friend Bildad suggested that, because of his troubles, he could not be considered a man of God. The hymn "I Know That My Redeemer Lives" (*LSB* 461) is based on Job's answer:

> Oh that my words were written! Oh that they were inscribed in a book! Oh that with an iron pen and lead

> they were engraved in the rock forever! For I know that my Redeemer lives, and at the last He will stand upon the earth. And after my skin has been thus destroyed, yet in my flesh I shall see God, whom I shall see for myself, and my eyes shall behold, and not another. My heart faints within me! (Job 19:23–27)

No matter what struggles we face in life, we can hold on to the positive truth that Jesus is our Redeemer, that He died for us and rose again, that He is coming again in glory and will raise us from the dead, and that we will see Him with our own eyes. There is no mistake about that.

Paul also gives an example of a Christian about to die who was earnestly looking forward to the appearing of Christ at the end of time. "For I am already being poured out as a drink offering, and the time of my departure has come. I have fought the good fight, I have finished the race, I have kept the faith. Henceforth there is laid up for me the crown of righteousness, which the Lord, the righteous judge, will award to me on that Day, and not only to me but also to all who have loved His appearing" (2 Timothy 4:6–8). Notice that everyone who looks forward to the coming of the Lord is receiving the crown. And I know, Lloyd, that you are looking forward to that great day. That's the day when you will see Jesus.

Lloyd did not get to hear the last two letters. He lapsed into a coma after Letter 89 and did not hear of the Final Judgment and the blessed reunion we will enjoy in heaven. I suppose it doesn't matter that Lloyd did not hear these things from me. He was well-prepared for the judgment and the blessed reunion as he found himself enjoying the presence of Jesus and the consummation of the promise that those who are left until the coming of the Lord will in no way precede those who have fallen asleep in Christ. And Lloyd, without having heard so from me, would content himself with actually seeing, hearing, and feeling the embrace of his Father who, for Christ's sake, welcomes one more prodigal into His heavenly home.

◇◇◇◇

Judgment Day

Letter 89

When Christ returns in glory, He will judge both the living and the dead. The judgment is described in Matthew 25 and other places. Those who died will be raised from the dead. Those who are still alive when Jesus comes "will be caught up together with them in the clouds to meet the Lord in the air" (1 Thessalonians 4:17). Then Jesus will go about the lengthy process of judgment.

Jesus will separate the sheep (those whom God has chosen, declared righteous, and blessed with the Gospel) from the goats (those who have steadfastly refused to believe in Jesus). He will commend the sheep for all the things they have done to help others in need. "As you did it to one of the least of these My brothers, you did it to Me" (Matthew 25:40). Then He will condemn those who did not do loving things for others and consign them to hell, which was prepared for the devil and his angels.

A Christian woman once told me that she was fearful of Judgment Day because she was worried that everyone would hear about all the wrong and apparently shameful things she had done. I know that if everyone knew about my most shameful and secret sins I would be pretty embarrassed. But God will not point out any of the sins of His sheep on the Last Day. All the sins you have confessed to God, Lloyd, have been long since forgotten by Jesus. And even the sins you have not remembered to confess have been washed by the blood of the Lamb.

But it's not just that God won't say anything bad about you. He will say plenty of good. You will be commended. His commendation will center in the vocation He has given us. It's as if He is saying, "Look what I am able to produce in sinners when I take over their lives."

It might take quite a while for God to point out all the good works of all the Christians, but it's not as though we will be constrained by anyone's schedule.

This Day of Judgment will end with God bringing you into His kingdom.

The Blessed Reunion

Letter 90

When Jesus comes again at the resurrection, we will experience something the Church has called "the blessed reunion." There is a beautiful and touching story in the Book of 2 Samuel that gives us an example of that reunion.

David had committed adultery with Bathsheba. He had slept with her while her husband was out with David's army. Bathsheba became pregnant. David tried to cover his sin but to no avail. So he had Bathsheba's husband, Uriah, killed. Then he went and married Bathsheba, who later gave birth to a son. Subsequently, Nathan the prophet then came to David, made him realize the inexcusable nature of his offense, listened to his confession, and pronounced upon him the absolution, "the LORD also has put away your sin" (2 Samuel 12:13).

From the seed of David, as you probably know, God was going to provide His Messiah, who would save the world. And there could be no doubt that any child born to David was legally his. The child born to Bathsheba was not legally David's because she had conceived while married to Uriah. So the child became very sick and David was alarmed. It says that he pleaded with God, he fasted, he spent his nights lying on the ground, and he refused to eat. All this was so that God would be gracious to him and let the child live. When the child died, his servants were afraid to tell David because they thought that he would be inconsolable. He noticed them whispering and asked directly if the child had died. When they answered affirmatively he got up, washed, ate, changed his clothes, and went into the house of the Lord to worship.

The servants couldn't understand his behavior. When asked, he replied, "While the child was still alive, I fasted and wept, for I said, 'Who knows whether the LORD will be gracious to me . . . ?' But now he is dead. Why should I fast? Can I bring him back again? I shall go to him, but he will not return to me" (2 Samuel 12:22–23).

"I will go to him, but he will not return to me." David understood the permanent nature of death. You can't come back from the dead. Why would anyone want to if they were with Jesus? But David also knew that someday he would go to heaven, and he would be reunited with his infant son.

So when you go to heaven, Lloyd, you will have a blessed reunion. You will see your dear departed wife, Edith. She will say, "What kept you?" You will see all those who "have fallen asleep in the Lord." You will see all the saints who have gone to heaven before you, though, when you think about it, we will all arrive at the same time because we will all be raised from the dead at the same time. Read those passages I quoted from Revelation three letters ago. All the people in heaven are together—a great multitude—singing to God, enjoying His company, and the eternal fellowship of Christ and all Christians.

So conclude my letters to Lloyd, who died early Sunday morning on Epiphany, January 6, 2008.

Nine months earlier, when I drove from Fresno to San Francisco on that crisp March day of 2007, I saw Lloyd for the last time. But I know that I will see him again someday. When Christ comes in His glory, we will both bow before His throne. We will both eat with joy the fruit from the tree of life, which is our Lord. We will both sing the song He gave us: "To Him who sits on the throne and to the Lamb be blessing and honor and glory and might forever and ever!" (Revelation 5:13).

Perhaps as we sing, we will catch each other's eyes across that heavenly sanctuary. I imagine that we will each mouth the words "Thank you"; he for the word I was privileged to write, and I for the opportunity to write to someone who was so eager to listen.

I also imagine that as he is introduced to the millions of saints who confessed the name of Christ, perhaps a handful might say to him, "You're Lloyd. I read about you in those letters. Nice to see you here with Jesus."

Evangelism Principles

As I reflect upon the eighteen months of letters, it occurs to me that I was doing the work of an evangelist and at the same time arguing the case of Christ to a friend—the two seem to be pretty much the same. And as I reflect further, it becomes apparent that certain evangelistic principles presented themselves that I followed, though at the time I was just trying to write the Word of God to Lloyd as best I could.

1. It is better to talk to one person ten times than ten persons once.

I am convinced that Lloyd became a Christian because he kept hearing the Word of God over and over again from one person. Others did talk to him, and I'm certain that God worked in those conversations as well. God works through His Word regardless of who speaks it or writes it. I really had no control over what others said. All I could do was write to him often. So that is what I did.

I had spoken the Gospel to Lloyd intermittently during the decade I had known him before 2006. But it wasn't until I began to speak to him regularly with the Word over a period of time that the Word actually took root and bore fruit.

"Effective" evangelism, if there is such a thing, does not occur during thirty-minute conversations between strangers on doorsteps. It occurs when Christians talk to their loved ones over and over again. It happens when people are allowed to ask questions and receive answers. It occurs when our sense of urgency bows to the painstaking task of conversing over a long period of time.

2. Before someone will listen to the message of Christ, their objections to the message must be addressed.

After his "deathbed" conversation with me, I was convinced that Lloyd would not seriously listen to the Gospel of Christ until his questions about miracles and the virgin birth were answered. So my first letters addressed his concerns. I was not able to offer a coherent presentation of the Gospel until the sixth letter, and I was not certain Lloyd would live much past the first five letters. But what was I to do? The man had doubts about miracles. He needed a thorough explanation of why it is not irrational to believe in the possibility of miracles. I was not going to show him disrespect by foisting my agenda on him. Rather, I let him set the agenda and patiently waited for the chance to speak more directly of Christ than his initial questions allowed.

Later Lloyd came back with some additional questions, which suggested that he believed some of the "Time Warner" theology as I labeled it. This is theology that you get from popular, shallow, and non-Christian magazines or television shows. Despite my eagerness to move the conversation to a discussion of the implications of the cross, I had to write Letters 12 and 13. These two interrupt the flow of my presentation and seem to have been inserted awkwardly into the discussion. That's because they were. I am convinced that Lloyd would not have paid much attention to the discussion about the resurrection if I had not taken the time and effort to answer his questions.

I always answered Lloyd's questions before I proceeded with what I felt was crucial. His questions were crucial to him. They became crucial to me.

Evangelists answer questions. Letters 1–20 and 65–68 are examples of answering questions in the course of conversations about Christ.

3. Objections are not usually stated unless a level of trust is achieved.

Lloyd trusted me. I always treated him with respect and I loved his daughter. Further, I always acted as though Christianity was the most normal thing in the world to talk about and the most normal thing not to talk about. It was neither the forbidden topic of conversation nor the subject matter that was forced down his throat. So when we finally were able to have a theological discussion, it was neither forced nor contrived. We just conversed in a normal way. Because of that trust, Lloyd was honest with me. He honestly didn't believe in miracles. He didn't worry about my disapproval when he revealed his lack of faith. He knew I would still love him and still treat him respectfully no matter what he believed. When he did reveal his lack of faith, it gave me something to say.

How does an evangelist present the Gospel in such a way that the other person will listen? If the other person trusts you, he will listen. People will listen or read more attentively if their concerns, sins, life situation, fears, or objections are addressed. And for the preacher or evangelist to know these concerns or objections, he must earn the trust of those to whom he speaks.

My conversation with Lloyd on March 2007 was a wonderful evangelistic event in every sense of the word. I was able to tell Lloyd that Jesus has fulfilled the obligations of the Law in his place, that He counts this obedience to his credit, and that He wanted Lloyd to give up all pretensions at his own capacity to fulfill God's Law. I could talk that way because I enjoyed the type of relationship with Lloyd that made him trust me.

Evangelists know that they work better in an environment of trust. Letters that demonstrate that trust had been developed are 4, 22, and 57.

4. False doctrine must be contradicted.

False doctrine is teaching something which conflicts with the teachings of the Scripture. False doctrine either makes the Law less severe than God intends it or, worse, makes the Gospel more difficult than God wants it by adding conditions to it. False doctrine is never benign.

When Lloyd was confronted with a particular false doctrine as recounted in Letter 38 and following, I knew that I had to speak against the false doctrine. This was necessary not simply because I enjoy being correct; rather, because Lloyd's faith was in jeopardy.

How the various articles of the Gospel are addressed I suppose was a bit risky since Lloyd was a very easygoing man. He would bend over backwards to avoid conflict. And here I was contradicting a very nice person, howbeit a false teacher, who had visited him. At the same time, I recalled Jesus, who directly contradicted the Samaritan woman for her bad theology and she ended up being converted to faith in Him. The Bible tells us to "watch out for" and "avoid" those "who cause divisions and create obstacles contrary to the doctrine you have been taught" (Romans 16:17). This was my way of applying this passage to Lloyd by teaching him to watch out for and avoid someone who was placing offensive teaching before him. Too much was at stake for me to say nothing. That's always the way it is with false doctrine.

No matter how unpleasant, true evangelists will always correct false doctrine when necessary. Letters 44–53 and 83 are examples of speaking against false doctrine.

5. You have to risk speaking the Law.

The Law of God is His just and holy demand upon us to be committed to Him alone above all things and to act in consistent and unfailing love toward our neighbor. The Law is summarized in the Ten Commandments. It does more than instruct us about what is right and wrong. The Law kills us. It always accuses. It strips us naked before the judgment throne of God and exposes our nature and offenses to Him who judges justly. It makes us see that by nature we are wholly unable and even unwilling to trust God as we ought and to love others as He wills. The Law causes excruciating pain. And the Law does not always bring out the best in us.

I did not want to alienate Lloyd by making him angry over the Law. Yet the Law must be spoken. No one in the history of the world has become and remained a Christian without knowing the searing pain of God as He cuts us and kills us with His just Law. And the true evangelist knows that God's Law must do its work, however risky, in order for the Gospel to be heeded. "Those who are well have no need of a physician, but those who are sick," says our Lord (Luke 5:31). He did not come for the righteous but for sinners.

So I had to make Lloyd spiritually sick before he would listen to the Great Physician. Lloyd needed to be self-critical. He had to question and deny both his opinions and his actions, which were barriers to his hearing the Gospel. So, I made him question the manner in which he had attempted to regain his faith. I made him question the rationality of his denial of miracles. My entire first ten letters were written to force him to conclude that he was wrong, unreasonable, and in danger. The first ten letters were written to give me the right to ask, "When you die, Lloyd, what will happen?" This was written to scare Lloyd, as only the Law can do. It was intended to make him want to hear the Gospel.

After I visited Lloyd in March 2007, it seemed apparent to me that he was no longer questioning miracles as much as the devastating and ego-destroying import of the Law itself. He was like the rich young lawyer, stubbornly trying to figure out alternatives to true faith. Should he give away all earthly wealth in order to attain heavenly wealth? So I wrote Letters 58–62, which are almost exclusively Law, and at times rather personal, to show Lloyd that he was unworthy of any of God's gracious blessings. I suppose I risked trust in order to kill him with the Law. But the risk was worth it.

Risky as it may seem, evangelists learn to speak the Law. Letters 58–62 are examples of harsh law.

6. The Gospel must be spoken in many ways.

The Gospel is not a message that can be easily summarized in four easy-to-memorize sentences or presented in ten simple steps or principles.

The Gospel is the Good News of Christ. It is something so simple you can have it in vessels on the altar or in a bowl at the font. It is so childlike it can be summarized in three words: "Jesus loves me." Yet it is something so intricate that the greatest theologians in history have never grasped its every nuance nor articulated it with all its brilliance.

The Gospel is the news that the guilty are acquitted, the lost are found, the estranged are reconciled, the slaves are redeemed, the spiritually poor are made rich with grace, the dead are raised, and those who have always been lacking will feast with the Lord in heaven. The Gospel applies to all—to infants and to men who are 92 years old.

The Gospel is a diamond with a thousand facets of God's promise in Christ, each true and each life-giving. Certain facets provide God's gracious response to different individuals, situations, or eras. It is no mystery that during times of persecution the Books of Revelation or 1 Peter gain greater attendance by God's Church. And in our post-modern era, Paul's stark assertions in Galatians or systematic presentation in Romans have a stronger appeal than other Scriptures might. So an individual depending on his background, experiences, and sins, might understand or appreciate one facet of the Gospel more than another.

As I look back at the letters I wrote, I recognize that the certainty of the promise was emphasized when Lloyd seemed doubtful. When he started going back to church, I wrote about the Word and Sacrament. When tempted by false doctrine, Lloyd needed to hear the assurance of grace alone because false doctrine denies grace alone. When he felt his guilt, then Law and Gospel prevailed. When he joined a church, then an explanation of the Apostles' Creed seemed fitting. And when death was imminent, a discussion of heaven was appropriate. It was all Gospel. And Lloyd heard almost all of it. I would suspect that some of the letters hit the mark more than others. And if others read the letters, they will resonate more with some than others. The more facets of the Gospel a person hears and believes, the more secure is their faith and the more comfort and joy they have in Christ.

Also by the Author

Books

The Fire and the Staff: Lutheran Theology in Practice (St. Louis: Concordia Publishing House, 2004).

Articles

"Tongues: An Evaluation from a Scientific Perspective." *Concordia Theological Quarterly* 46:4 (1982): 277.

"Jonathan Edwards: A Case of Medium-Message Conflict." *Concordia Theological Quarterly* 48:4 (1984): 279.

"Contemporary Christian Music: An Evaluation." *Concordia Theological Quarterly* 51:1 (1987): 1.

"The Theology of the Church Growth Movement: An Evaluation of Kent Hunter's 'Confessions.'" *Logia* 10:1 (Epiphany 2001).

"The Difference between Evangelical and Lutheran Preaching in America." *The Pieper Lectures: Preaching through the Ages*, ed. John A. Maxfield, Concordia Historical Institute (2004).

"Kyrios or Kairos." *Logia* 16:1 (2007).

"Pietism in Missouri's Mission: From the Mission Affirmations to *Ablaze!*" *Congress on the Lutheran Confessions: Mission Accomplished?* ed. John A. Maxfield, The Luther Academy (2008).

"Personal Holiness." *Congress on the Lutheran Confessions: We Confess, We Condemn*, ed. John A. Maxfield, The Luther Academy (2009).

"Doctrine and Practice: Resisting the Influence of Evangelicalism." *Logia* 18:2 (2009).

Further Reading

Chemnitz, Martin. *The Lord's Prayer.* Translated by Georg Williams. St. Louis: Concordia, 2000.

D'Souza, Dinesh. *What's So Great About Christianity.* Washington DC: Regnery, 2007.

Harrison, Matthew C., *Christ Have Mercy: How to Put Your Faith in Action.* St. Louis: Concordia, 2008.

Kinnaman, Scot A., ed. *Lutheranism 101.* St. Louis: Concordia, 2010.

Kolb, Robert. *Speaking the Gospel Today.* St. Louis: Concordia, 1984, 1995.

Maier, Paul L. *The Very First Easter.* St. Louis: Concordia, 2004.

McDowell, Josh. *Evidence That Demands A Verdict.* Nashville: Thomas Nelson, 1999.

Parton, Craig A. *The Defense Never Rests: A Lawyer's Quest for the Gospel.* St. Louis: Concordia, 2003.

Pless, John T. *Handling the Word of Truth: Law and Gospel in the Church Today.* St. Louis: Concordia, 2004.

Preus, Daniel. *Why I Am a Lutheran: Jesus at the Center.* St. Louis: Concordia, 2004.

Preus, Herman A. *A Theology to Live By: The Practical Luther for the Practicing Christian.* St. Louis: Concordia, 2005

Senkbeil, Harold L. *Dying to Live: The Power of Forgiveness.* St. Louis: Concordia, 1994.

Sproul, R. C. *Reason to Believe: A Response to Common Objections to Christianity.* Grand Rapids: Zondervan, 1982.

Veith, Gene Edward, Jr. *The Spirituality of the Cross: The Way of the First Evangelicals.* St. Louis: Concordia, 2010.

Notes

LETTER 13

1. William Whiston, trans. *Josephus: Complete Works*, (Grand Rapids: Kregel Publications, 1960), book XVIII, chapter III, paragraph 3, 379.
2. Lucian, "The Passing of Peregrinus." (Translated from the Greek by Dan Jastram.)
3. Cornelius, *Tacitus Annals*, XV 44. (Translated from the Latin by Josh Christian.)
4. Pliny the Younger, Epistle X.96. (Translated from the Latin by Josh Christian.)
5. Pliny the Younger, Epistle X.96. (Translated from the Latin by Josh Christian.)

LETTER 48

6. George M. Marsden, *Fundamentalism and American Culture: The Shaping of Twentieth Century Evangelicalism: 1870–1925* (New York: Oxford University Press, 1980), 45. Used by permission of Oxford University Press, USA.

Topical Index

Who is the Lloyd in your life?

A short note, a Scripture verse, a word of encouragement—all of these are easy ways to share Christ with your family and friends and open up lines of communication.

These inspirational postcards are provided for you to take that first step. Use them to prayerfully reach out to those who need to hear God's saving word.

Are there more people you would like to share the Word with?

Visit **cph.org/sharingchrist** to send free e-cards.